T0301807

Multi-Stakeholder Decision Making for Complex Problems

A Systems Thinking Approach with Cases

Multi-Stakeholder Decision Making for Complex Problems

A Systems Thinking Approach with Cases

Kambiz Maani

Massey University, New Zealand

 **World Scientific**

EW JERSEY · LONDON · SINGAPORE · BEIJING · SHANGHAI · HONG KONG · TAIPEI · CHENNAI · TOKYO

Published by

World Scientific Publishing Co. Pte. Ltd.

5 Toh Tuck Link, Singapore 596224

USA office: 27 Warren Street, Suite 401-402, Hackensack, NJ 07601

UK office: 57 Shelton Street, Covent Garden, London WC2H 9HE

Library of Congress Cataloging-in-Publication Data

Names: Maani, Kambiz E., author.

Title: Multi-stakeholder decision making for complex problems : a systems thinking approach with cases / Kambiz Maani.

Description: New Jersey : World Scientific, [2016]

Identifiers: LCCN 2015048901 | ISBN 9789814619738

Subjects: LCSH: Decision making. | System analysis. | Problem solving.

Classification: LCC HD30.23 .M25 2016 | DDC 658.4/032--dc23

LC record available at http://lccn.loc.gov/2015048901

British Library Cataloguing-in-Publication Data

A catalogue record for this book is available from the British Library.

Desk Editor: Shreya Gopi

Typeset by Stallion Press

Email: enquiries@stallionpress.com

Printed in Singapore

To my father, Misagh, a great teacher who taught us the love of learning.

Contents

The unleashed power of the atom has changed everything save our modes of thinking, and we thus drift toward unparalleled catastrophes.

Albert Einstein

Preface

Despite sophisticated technology, educated managers, and the best of intentions, business and government decisions are fraught with failures and unintended consequences. These decisions impact our economy, environment, society, and communities, locally and globally (e.g., the Global Financial Crisis, the BP oil spill in the Gulf of Mexico). This suggests a glaring absence of fresh and scientifically-based tools for decision making in complex scenarios.

At the same time, most problems are complex, or "wicked". These problems, like the environment, poverty, international security, finance, food shortages, and water crises, defy conventional single-dimension approaches.

In a connected and dynamic world, complex decision making involves engaging with multiple stakeholders, operating in different domains, with competing interests, differing perspectives, and conflicting agendas under uncertain and often adversarial conditions. Worse, long delays and feedback cycles inherent in complex systems exacerbate decisions and their anticipated outcomes, causing adverse unintended consequences.

Today, local problems and global challenges cannot be viewed and solved with narrow, reductionist mindsets and the tools developed from such mindsets. Leaders and decision makers need to understand complexity and how to deal with it in the multi-stakeholder contexts that predominate today. In the words of a prominent public policy maker: "Tackling wicked problems… requires thinking that is capable of grasping the big picture, including the interrelationships among the full range of causal factors underlying them. They often require broader, more collaborative, and innovative approaches."[1]

Today, the unprecedented rate of knowledge creation and the vast range of disciplines involved in addressing complex problems make a compelling case for the integration of disparate knowledge, perspectives, and values for collective decision making. Ironically, however, the prevailing approaches to decision making are reductionist, isolated, and linear. Global challenges such as climate change, poverty, public health, and sustainability defy isolated solutions from a single science, discipline, expertise or agency. Rather, these challenges require a confluence of diverse domains and disciplines including social, cultural, political, financial, and *spiritual* considerations to achieve acceptable and sustainable outcomes.

This book draws from the author's more than two decades of working first-hand with hundreds of senior managers and CEOs, policy makers, scientists, postgraduate students, community leaders, and stakeholders in a wide range of private and public organizations. A vast volume of knowledge is condensed in a unique book synthesizing lessons learned and insights gained.

The book also introduces and demonstrates a range of practical tools and scientific methods that could assist thousands of decision makers and organizations to solve wicked problems. The book's core methodology, Systems Thinking, is explained in non-technical and lay language with a focus on multi-domain, multi-stakeholder decision making. In Part 2, the book demonstrates the Systems Thinking methodology through several real case studies in a wide range of areas including sustainability, climate change, agriculture, health policy, energy, and business strategy and planning. Hence, this book offers a timely, critical, and fresh approach for dealing with complex challenges facing today's evolving global society.

Kambiz Maani
Auckland
June 2016

---

[1]Australian Public Service Commission (2007), Tackling wicked problems: A public policy perspective, Australian Government.

Part 1
Concepts and Methods

Chapter 1

An Introduction to Multi-Stakeholder Decision Making

We cannot solve problems with the same mindset that created them.

Einstein

1.1 Introduction

As you read these pages, the world is growing ever more complex, confused, and unpredictable.

Complexity characterizes the world and all human endeavors today — in business, government, social, natural, scientific, and political spheres. Local problems and global challenges can no longer be viewed and solved with narrow, single dimensional mind-sets and tools. Leaders and decision makers need to understand complexity and how to deal with it in multi-stakeholder scenarios.

Systems Thinking is the science of integration. It provides a 'language' for decision makers, researchers, research managers, policy makers, and knowledge managers to understand complexity and multi-stakeholder problem solving. In addition, Systems Thinking processes engender problem-solving skills, team participation, and team learning.

Complexity arises out of interdependencies. Interdependency of relationships is the main source of complexity and complexity is the principal source of uncertainty and ensuing anxiety. Climate change, poverty, the water crisis, food quality and security, the environment, and similar 'big' issues are not just passing problems for governments, policy makers, and scientists. They are everyone's and every day's burden. Dealing with big issues, and even not-so-big ones, requires a different mode of interacting and decision making unlike any we have known before. Information and communication technologies are rapidly changing the modes of interacting. Social media is swiftly shifting the power to the masses, especially the young and educated. Mass movements are becoming the mainstays of social and political change.

The challenges leaders face today are greater than ever. No longer can a single leader be responsible for an organization's future. Everyone in a company, school, government agency, or community must take on the challenges and lead from their own position. But leading together in this way requires a special attitude and a special set of skills, including self-inquiry, shared vision, and Systems Thinking.[1]

1.2 Why Decisions Fail

Leaders, managers, and policy makers are often frustrated by a lack of consensus and collaboration on challenging issues — so they end up blaming outside factors or each other. Even setting aside special interests, hidden agendas, and ill-intentions, there is an alarming level of divergence and lack of a shared understanding of complex issues. This is highlighted by the fact that so many decisions made by very smart and highly educated managers and leaders in elite and sophisticated organizations often fail miserably, with far reaching and adverse consequences for everyone.

Peter Senge, the author of *The Fifth Discipline*, once said that "today's problems are yesterday's solutions". By the same token, a good number of today's interventions will become future problems. Is there a way to circumvent this common downside so that today's solutions don't end up as tomorrow's problems?

The discipline of Economics is grounded on the notion of 'rational' decision making. However, researchers in psychology, cognitive science,

---

[1] Systems Thinking in Action Conference Flyer, Pegasus Communications, Boston, 1995.

and management have found compelling evidence that refutes rational decision making. Noble Laureate economist and psychologist Hebert Simon dubbed 'bounded rationality' as a notion that explains why the human mind cannot process information and decode relationships beyond second or third level orders. In fact, the role of intuition and emotions in decision making is often overlooked in management 'science' and quantitative modeling. This is ironic as most people can relate to this intuitively. Only computers and robots could be expected to make rational and strictly rule-based decisions.

Based on his comprehensive study of human decision making, John Morecroft concludes that "there are severe limitations on the information processing and computing abilities of human decision makers. As a result, decision making can never achieve the ideal of perfect (objective) rationality, but is destined to a lower level of intended rationality."[2] He identified six common practices that underlie the shortcomings of the human decision-making process and which support bounded rationality. They are:

1. Factored (fragmented) decision making
   Complex issues are divided up into pieces (e.g., disciplines, sections, departments) to facilitate decision making, as "they cannot be handled by an individual".
2. Partial and certain information
   Decision makers tend to use "only a small proportion of the information that might be relevant to full consideration of a given situation". They also tend to discard uncertain information. This diverts the focus of the decisions to problem symptoms and locally optimum solutions.
3. Rules of thumb / Routine
   This refers to situations where decision makers, under time pressure, resort to "quick fixes" in order to rectify a situation as quickly as possible. Quick fixes often "backfire" or result in unintended outcomes.
4. Narrow goals and incentives
   A focus on narrow goals and incentives compromises other areas and undermines the performance of the larger system.

---

[2]Morecroft, J. (1983) "System dynamics: Portraying bounded rationality". *OMEGA* 11(2): 131–142.

5. Authority and culture
   Culture and tradition provide powerful predetermined frameworks for decision makers (i.e., mind-set, mental model). Through customary routines and commands, prevailing values and traditions are transmitted to all and thus get reinforced and become further ingrained.
6. Basic cognitive processes
   "People take time to collect and transmit information. They take still more time to absorb information, process it, and arrive at a judgment. There are limits to the amount of information they can manipulate and retain. These cognitive processes can introduce delay, distortion, and bias into information channels."[3]

Other researchers have identified further factors that lead to poor managerial decision making, including[4]:

- Presence of multiple actors (stakeholders) in decision making,
- Lack of understanding of feedback in complex systems,
- Lack of appreciation of non-linearity, and
- Hidden time delays

Hence decision making about complex problems fails for many reasons. Human behavior and lack of understanding are not the sole reasons why decision making about wicked problems fails. The nature of the problems also contributes to unsatisfactory outcomes.

1.3 Wicked, Messy Problems

For every complex question there is a simple answer, and it is wrong.[5]

From a young age we have been taught in school that there's only one correct answer to a problem. However, most real-world problems are 'wicked' and defy this maxim. Horst Rittel and Melvin M. Webber, Professors in

---

[3] Ibid.
[4] Sterman, J. (1989) "Modeling managerial behavior: misperceptions of feedback in a dynamic decision making experiment." *Management Science* 35(3): 321–339.
[5] *Business Week* 21 April 1980, p. 25.

Design and City Planning respectively, coined the term 'wicked problems'. Later, Richard Buchanan defined wicked problems succinctly[6]:

> A class of social problems which are ill-formulated, where the information is confusing, where there are many clients and decision makers with conflicting values, and where the ramifications in the whole system are thoroughly confusing.

Wicked problems arise in any situation involving multiple stakeholders where the following characteristics are present:

1. The solution depends on how the problem is framed and vice-versa (i.e., the problem definition depends on the solution).
2. Stakeholders have radically different world views and different frames for understanding the problem.
3. The constraints that the problem is subject to and the resources needed to solve it change over time.
4. The problem is never solved definitively.[7]

Russell Ackoff, a renowned systems scholar, refers to these as 'messy problems' — situations in which there are large differences of opinion about the problem or even on the question of whether there is a problem. Thus, messy problems are ill-structured situations that make it difficult for decision makers and stakeholders to reach agreement.

There are two sources of messy problems, the individual and the group or team situations. Limited information processing capacity and entrenched mental models are the main contributors to the individual sources of messy problems. In particular, mental models are powerful drivers of behavior as they shape the perception of reality.[8]

The group sources of messy problems relate to the dynamics of their interaction and the tendency of members to defend or promote their own

---

[6]Buchanan, R. (1992) "Wicked problems in design thinking." *Design Issues* 8(2): 5–21.
[7]Rittel, Horst W. J.; Melvin M. Webber (1973) "Dilemmas in a general theory of planning", *Policy Sciences*, **4**: 155–169.
[8]Vennix, J. A. M. (1999) "Group model-building: Tackling messy problems." *System Dynamics Review*, 15: 379–401.

self-interest in decision-making situations. Often the difficulties in group interaction are exacerbated by lack of independent investigation on the part of team members and the manner of their communication.

The nature of wicked, messy problems described in the preceding paragraphs highlights the role of an independent and experienced facilitator in multi-stakeholder decision-making situations. A facilitator should have no stake in the outcomes of decisions and should be able to moderate negative dynamics and quell tensions in the group. A facilitator who uses Systems Thinking tools such as conceptual mapping and computer modeling, clarifies and aligns disparate mental models to create a 'shared understanding' of complex problems within a diverse group. Lack of a shared understanding is the missing element in most multi-stakeholder situations where decision makers tend to 'jump into solutions' without an adequate understanding of the problem and its broader social context. In this regard, Senge suggests that Systems Thinking interventions will be much more effective if they are skillfully combined with expert facilitation.[9]

1.4 Pitfalls in Decision Making

In their multi-year research project and experiments with thousands of managers, Maani and Li identified seven common pitfalls in decision making.[10] Li also studied these pitfalls empirically using simulation models in a laboratory setting.[11]

1. Don't do brain surgery when you get a headache

Managers and policy makers tend to 'over-intervene'. Over-reaction (intervention) is common practice in policy making and management. The common mind-set is that launching many initiatives is a good thing. However, most managers are not conscious that multi-interventions can

---

[9] Senge, P. (1991) *The Fifth Discipline — The Art & Practice of The Learning Organization.* Adelaide, Random House.

[10] Maani, K, Li, A. (2006) *Counter Intuitive Managerial Behaviour in Complex Systems,* ISSS Conference, Sonoma, CA.

[11] Li, A. (2007) *Decision-Making and Interventions in Complex Systems,* PhD Thesis, The University of Auckland.

cause *unintended consequences*. This is caused and amplified by a lack of understanding of cause-and-effect and misperception of dynamics within a system. Every time someone does something, it triggers or influences more than one thing. A new solution or initiative can set in motion a chain reaction that could counteract and create counterintuitive, and often worse, outcomes than what had been expected. This behavior manifests itself in various ways, such as micro-management, over-reaction, and tampering. Jim Collins, the author of *Good to Great*[12] advises that for every to do list, decision makers should have a "not to do list". The temptation for doing something else often overwhelms the wisdom for *not* doing anything.

Influence versus Change

Headaches are common, but no one will do brain surgery to cure a headache. What we normally do is 'influence' the biology of the body (the system) to treat the headache. The headache tablet releases special chemicals into the blood stream, which after some time begin to change the chemical imbalance that is causing the headache. This is the difference between change and influence.

2. Not everything that counts can be counted

Decision makers and managers commonly ignore 'soft' variables to the detriment of the employees and their organizations. This is a failure to recognize that soft indicators are *leading* indicators of individual and organizational behavior and performance. Soft variables are subtle and 'invisible' yet they are powerful factors that influence the dynamics within groups and organizations. Things such as trust, morale, time pressure, stress, burnout, commitment, loyalty, confidence, jealousy, and fear can be regarded as measures of internal *health* and vitality of an organization. Soft variables can be powerful predictors of long-term performance.

In an extensive empirical study of decision making,[13] only 20% of the subjects acknowledged "time pressure" as a factor that could

---

[12]Collins, J. (2001) *Good to Great*, Harper Collins Publishers.
[13]Li, A. (2007) *Decision-Making and Interventions in Complex Systems*, PhD Thesis, The University of Auckland.

potentially affect staff performance in their strategies. A mere 3% of this group (0.06% of all subjects) *proactively* managed time pressure as a critical performance measure. This highlights that the great majority of decision makers in the study were oblivious to or ignored the effect of time pressure on staff performance.

3. Delays are dangerous

Decision makers are often unaware of the effect of "time delays" on decision outcomes. Lack of attention to systemic delays undermines performance and inhibits system stability. We experience this daily when we take a shower. We start by turning the tap to the hot water, but it takes time (delay) for the hot water to arrive. During this short delay period, in order to get the hot water faster, we turn the tap further. But when the water arrives it is scalding hot, which forces us to quickly reverse the tap. This example shows interventions or overreactions during delays can make a system unstable. Sterman has shown this "bullwhip" effect through his famous beer distribution game — through multiple stages of a supply chain, when inventory managers fear delay of supply, they overreact and order more supply only to create a huge over supply of beer and unneeded inventories.[14]

In his experiments of managerial decision making, Li found that nearly half of his subjects showed awareness of systems delays. However, while the majority of this group anticipated delays, only 4% of the sample had actively included provisions for mitigating delay in their strategies — for example, hiring more workers early on to offset the up-to-speed delay, while keeping production goals at a lower level to ease off the time pressure.

4. Beware of too many KPIs

Organizations tend to use too many micro and sometimes conflicting performance measures (i.e., KPIs). Since the nature and number of KPIs impacts performance, excessive and inappropriate performance measures can lead to trade-offs, poor outcomes, and unintended consequences.

---

[14]Sterman, J. D. (2000) *Business Dynamics — Systems Thinking and Modeling for a Complex World*, McGraw-Hill, Irwin.

5. Timing and sequence of actions

Managers tend to focus on actions only, or what needs to be done, but not so much on the timing and sequences of actions. Li's research shows that *timing* and *sequence* of actions are as important as the actions themselves and could make or break the outcomes of decisions.[15]

6. Worse before better

Judging performance by short-term results can be counterproductive. Decision makers and managers often judge performance by short-term results to the detriment of the organization in the long term. Quarterly financial reporting of stock prices is a prime example. Judging the performance and health of a complex entity such as an organization by its short-term results is like taking a new plant out of the soil to check the growth of its roots!

Studies show that immediately after an improvement initiative or program, performance often declines before it improves. This is because improvement initiatives, like quality management programs, disturb the organization (system) out of balance before it settles back to stability at higher performance levels. However, this causes decision makers to 'panic' and stop or reverse the initiative, sometimes at a considerable cost. Thus, a focus on short-term results can be misleading and can lead to counteracting outcomes.

7. Dramatic versus slow change

It is a common illusion that dramatic results come from dramatic actions — that radical change initiatives create better results. This misguided tendency comes from the misperception of links between cause and effect. The prevailing assumption is that a leader's role and legacy is to make dramatic changes. Contrary to this, history shows that lasting transformations come from modest and 'slow' actions and interventions that are patiently sustained over time.

---

[15]Li, A. (2007) *Decision-Making and Interventions in Complex Systems*, PhD Thesis, The University of Auckland.

This is best demonstrated in Collins seminal *Good to Great* book.[16] Collins and his research team at Stanford studied the performance of over 1,400 "good" companies using 40 years of data. Out of this group, they identified a mere 11 organizations that had successfully transformed themselves from good to great. Collins and his research team closely scrutinized the change/improvement strategies of these companies and identified a set of unique styles of "change" that underpin the success of the great companies.

The study challenged several 'myths' about change management, including the beliefs that: (1) big change has to be extreme and (2) breakthroughs can be achieved by using technology to leapfrog the competition. Neither of these myths was found in the 11 companies that managed to transform from good to great. Collins makes two analogies to illustrate how effective change happens.

The Egg (transformative change is not visible)

Transformation of an egg into a chick or a caterpillar into a butterfly is a slow and invisible process, and only the last step is an observable event (e.g,, the cracking of the egg shell). Organizations are not exempt from the rule of invisible but transformational change. Nevertheless, in organizations, changes are often perceived and measured in terms of tangible steps and outputs. However, "If a company is focusing on achieving just the 'shell cracking' moment, then it is not likely to succeed."[17]

The Flywheel (slow but persistent action counts)

To get a new initiative off the ground requires a tremendous amount of effort. An airplane needs maximum thrust and energy during takeoff. A heavy flywheel needs a huge amount of force to get started, but once it starts to move the wheel reinforces its own motion through momentum. Likewise in organizations, small and persistent interventions will ultimately bear fruits as "change and success will reinforce itself, without the requirement of big efforts or dramatic

---

[16]Collins, J. (2001) *Good to Great*, Harper Collins Publishers.
[17]Ibid.

interventions. In contrast, over-hyped change programs often fail, since they lack accountability, they fail to achieve credibility, and they have no authenticity. It's the opposite of the Flywheel Effect; it's the Doom Loop."[18]

The previous sections have described both human-based and problem-based challenges to solving complex problems. Decision makers who confront wicked problems need a tool set that ensures today's solutions do not become tomorrow's problems. One useful methodology to apply in these situations is multi-stakeholder decision making, a methodology derived from System Thinking and which is introduced in the next section.

1.5 Multi-Stakeholder Decision Making (MSDM)

Today nearly all significant social, political, and organizational problems are multi-stakeholder. For these problems no individual or group has all the answers as there are multiple 'truths' depending on one's past experiences and current reality. Hence, diverse insights and alternative points of view are imperative. As decision making becomes more collective and inclusive, the need for participatory, collaborative, and integrative approaches becomes more apparent and urgent. This is the core of Multi-Stakeholder Decision Making (MSDM). MSDM requires fresh perspectives and principles for inclusive engagements of all participants and which compromise should give way to consensus and win-win outcomes. The following principles are underlying characteristics of MSDM. Success of multi-stakeholder decision making depends on a genuine use and adherence to these principles.

1. **Participation**: Early participation and involvement of key stakeholders across functions, organizations, and sectors is crucial. This will facilitate ownership and commitment of the participants to group decisions. In this regard, mental models (e.g., values, beliefs, assumptions) and emotions of all participants must be understood and respected by other participants.

---

[18] Ibid.

2. **Common good outcomes**: It is critical for the facilitator to establish at the outset that the objective of the decision exercise is to reach the 'best' possible collective (common good) outcome, which means tradeoffs are inevitable and 'optimum' solutions that suit everyone are not realistic.

3. **Learning posture**: The decision-making process should be viewed as a learning process as complex problems evade simple, linear, and expert-driven approaches.

4. **Systemic understanding**: The first step should be to establish a systemic understanding of the problem and its environment within the group. The focus should then turn to finding systemic solutions (leverage points) rather than focusing on problem symptoms and short-term fixes.

5. **Leverage**: Leverage means one must look for interventions that change the system, not the symptoms. Often, lasting solutions are not the most obvious ones (e.g., educating women could be the best intervention for eradication of poverty).

6. **Timeframe**: Both short-term (symptomatic) and long-term (fundamental) interventions should be considered.

7. **Emergent outcomes**: The outcomes of decisions and plans are mostly unpredictable and will unravel over time in ways not always anticipated by decision makers. Thus interventions are best viewed as desirable directions for change and not as fixed and deterministic plans.

Facilitating multi-stakeholder decision making for solving wicked problems is not easy. Fortunately System Thinking has evolved to offer a number of perspectives and tools to address wicked problems in multi-stakeholder environments, and Systems Thinking is the focus of the next chapter.

Chapter 2

Systems Thinking

The whole is greater than the sum of its parts.

Aristotle

2.1 Introduction

To understand Systems Thinking we first need to understand "system". A system is a whole that is greater than the sum of its parts. This definition is not new, Aristotle said this about 350 BC! Russell Ackoff, a renowned systems scientist, put this in a more precise and powerful definition: A system is not the sum of its parts — it is the product of their interaction. To elaborate, Ackoff gives a simple but brilliant example. Bring a car in a large garage and disassemble it. As soon as you do that, you no longer have a car, although all the parts of the car are there in the garage. This is because a car is not the sum of its parts — it is the product of their interactions. Furthermore, once you disconnect the parts, they even lose their essential properties. In other words, they become useless and dysfunctional. Even the engine of the car, a system in and of itself, cannot move itself without being connected to other parts. Ackoff concludes "every system is defined by its role in a larger system".

Our body is another example; it is a biological system consisting of many 'parts' (cells, tissues, organs, *etc.*) Biological organs don't function in isolation, it is their harmonious connection and interaction that allows the body to stay alive and function. In Professor Ackoff's words, "it is not your hand that writes; it is *you* as a whole person that writes" (he asks to imagine what would happen if you cut off your hand and put it on table to see if it can write). Simply put, interconnectedness and interdependence are the hallmarks of all systems, from a living cell to the universe.

Not all interactions are positive or constructive. Some interactions within a system or between systems can become counterproductive and even destructive. In medicine, taking too many drugs or conflicting medications at the same time can produce negative effects — side effects or reactions that can be deadly. In chemistry, a combination of some elements can cause explosive or corrosive effects. In social groups like teams, marriages, and organizations, a 'wrong' combination of people can be counterproductive and even destructive.

Systems Thinking is increasingly recognized and applied as a powerful *paradigm* and *language* for thinking, understanding complexity, problem solving, and decision making. Morris L., *et al.* describes Systems Thinking as:

> Everywhere you look in the modern world you will see unintended consequences and outright systems failures... Systems Thinking offers two complementary sets of solutions for these situations. First, the discipline has developed a large body of knowledge about systems and how they really behave. Secondly, Systems Thinking keeps the focus on whole systems and the purposes for which they are designed so that people don't go so deeply lost in the details and lose sight of their overall purposes.[1]

This book introduces Systems Thinking as a scientific *language* for understanding, explaining, and solving endemic organizational and societal problems.

2.2 Knowledge versus Understanding

In daily conversations and decision making, we tend to use data, information, and knowledge interchangeably. However, Russell Ackoff

---

[1] Morris, L. *et al* (2004) ICSTM '04 Conference Summary & Synthesis, May, Philadelphia.

makes an important distinction amongst these, especially between knowledge and understanding. He describes the "contents of the mind" in five categories — data, information, knowledge, understanding, and wisdom.

— Data are the most basic level. They are facts and figures that are the building blocks of information and knowledge. Data can be stored, manipulated, and processed by computers.
— Information is the higher level of data where isolated pieces of data are combined into useable 'information'.
— Knowledge is about "how to" where combinations of relevant information leads to solving problems, discovering facts, and learning new ways.
— Understanding is the ability to grasp the "bigger picture" and deeper insights about relationships and interconnectedness amongst things.
— Wisdom is understanding the answer to "why" — the purpose and reason for doing things.

While data, information, and knowledge can be taught, learned, and transferred, understanding and wisdom require a different kind of 'learning' as knowledge alone cannot lead to understanding and wisdom. Some will never find that elusive wisdom, despite all the acquired knowledge. A doctor who is well aware (has knowledge) of smoking hazards may well be a smoker. A respected leader may risk his/her position with an illicit affair. Most people have knowledge of unhealthy food, but that does not stop most of us from eating it.

Systems Thinking provides the ability and skills to see the big picture, to view a problem with a wider lens, to unravel hidden relationships and interconnections, and to bring to the surface veiled assumptions and mental models. This creates new understanding and deeper insights that are most crucial in multi-stakeholder settings where divergent and conflicting views and perspectives abound. In these settings 'knowledge' itself can be a source of debate and dissension as different agents would hold different knowledge, whether scientific, experiential, cultural or indigenous. This is evident in most debates about climate change.

2.3 Systems versus Reductionist Approach

According to John Sterman, "Where the world is dynamic, evolving, and interconnected, we tend to make decisions using mental models that are static, narrow, and reductionist."[2] This is no more evident than in the key global issues facing the world. Daily we wake up to the news or a commentary on one of the crises of the 'day'. The list is long and includes terrorism, climate change, economic growth, poverty, environment, energy crisis, food crisis, water shortage, and globalization.

Typically, leaders, policy makers, scientists, NGOs, activists, and others deal with these issues *separately* and in isolation, normally through specialist agencies, ministries or departments. Ironically, no group or agency is charged to look at the big picture and the interdependencies and interactions amongst these issues. Yet, the relationships amongst these are rather obvious even to lay people. We intuitively know the connections between economic growth and poverty, climate change and the environment, and land use and water shortage. Less obvious are the links between energy and food crises, globalization and economic growth, and poverty and the environment.

While it is useful to deduce the interconnections amongst a group of variables, this does not provide the 'full picture' and the underlying dynamics amongst them. Systems Thinking focuses on the big picture (panoramic view) and the primacy of relationships. One of the tools of Systems Thinking, the Causal Loop Diagram (CLD), provides a scientific yet practical way to connect the pieces together to create a systems view of disparate variables. Figure 2.1 shows an example of a CLD for the global issues listed earlier. The first thing to notice is that most relationships in the model form a 'loop'. This is contrary to the common assumption of linearity. The fact is nothing in the world is linear. Linearity is only a mathematical assumption that we use for practical purposes such as measuring distance. In CLDs a closed loop denotes a feedback dynamic that is a natural part of all phenomena in the real world. (CLDs and feedback loops are more fully discussed later in this chapter.)

---

[2] Sterman, J. D. (2001) "System dynamics modeling: tools for learning in a complex world." *California Management Review*, 43(4), 8–25.

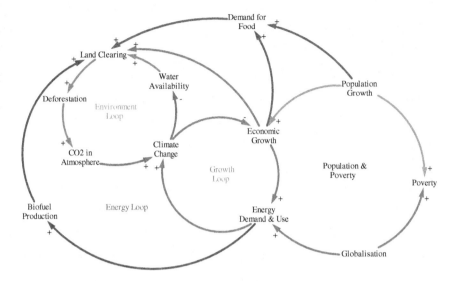

Figure 2.1. A systems model of world issues.

2.4 Systems Thinking and Strategic Planning

Planning is an important area of decision making. Traditional planning views the organization as a mechanical system and the purpose of planning is to shift the organization from position (or point) A to position B following a predictable straight path. With the world becoming more complex, chaotic, and unpredictable, this mechanistic approach to planning has become outdated and rather obsolete.

New theories of planning view the organization as a *living system* and planning as a *learning process* for organizational growth and transformation.[3] In particular, strategic planning is about thinking and preparing for the long term. By this virtue, strategic planning needs to integrate disparate areas and activities under a common framework. In this regard, Systems Thinking can be a powerful complement to strategic planning. However, while Systems Thinking and strategic planning share common features, there are notable differences between them. The following table contrasts strategic planning with Systems Thinking:

---

[3] De Geus, A.P., (2008) Planning as Learning, *Harvard Business Review*, 66(2), 70–74.

Table 2.1.   Strategic planning versus systems thinking.

Strategic planning	Systems thinking
• Once every 3–5 years	• Continuous
• Data driven	• Patterns and behavior over time trends
• Analysis	• Synthesis (cause-and-effect)
• Forecasting (a single fixed future)	• Scenarios (multiple possible futures)
• Focus on parts in isolation	• Focus on *interaction* of parts
• Linear	• Non-linear (closed causality and
• Predictable outcomes	feedback)
• Driven by expert/senior management	• Emergent outcomes
	• Participatory: management, staff, and stakeholders

Some of these differences are explained below.

• Planning is a specialist function

Planning in general, and strategic planning in particular, is treated as an internal and specialist function within the organization without active stakeholder/end-user participation. In larger organizations, strategic planning is regarded as a specialist and elite function — mainly the domain of senior managers and professional planners. Thus the great majority of the organization is disengaged from the planning process. While "environmental scanning" and other "externalities" are considered in some planning activities, active participation of wider internal and external stakeholders is largely absent in the planning process. This creates barriers to buy-in and commitment to the plan and risks its ultimate success.

• Planning implementation is flawed

Once a plan is developed and dispatched across the organization, it is *assumed* and *expected* that the plan document will be thoroughly read, understood, and followed as intended. In reality however, few managers and employees will unreservedly accept and follow the plan. In contrast, as MIT's John Sterman's extensive research shows, most organizational strategies and government policies produce "resistance" from the employees or the citizens.[4] Hence, strategies and policies 'backfire' or produce

---

[4] Sterman, J. D. (2001) "System dynamics modeling: tools for learning in a complex world." *California Management Review*, 43(4), 8–25.

unintended consequences. This is the greatest pitfall of planning, namely the gap between a plan and its actual implementation.

- Static world

Conventional planning is based on the implicit assumption of a constant and stable world — that the variables, parameters, and relationships that affect the plan are fixed at the time of planning and will remain so over the horizon of the plan.

While this assumption may have held true in the past, it is no longer tenable in a complex and dynamic world where predicting the future based on the past is shaky at best. Recent global crises such as the Global Financial Crisis, climate change, environment degradation, future energy supplies, food safety, bio-security, terrorism, and water shortages have starkly shown the fallacy of a static world. With rapid and accelerating rates of change, any planning exercise that does not incorporate dynamics is likely to disappoint.

- Linear thinking

This implicit assumption underlies most societal thinking and organizational planning — that cause and effect (change and outcomes) are proportional and hence predicable. Linear thinking has several scientific implications that betray simple cause-and-effect relationships. These are:

1. *Additivity*: the whole is equal to the sum of its parts.
2. *Proportionality*: changes in output are proportional to changes in input, forever. For example an increase in market share and sales would result in a concomitant increase in profit.
3. *Replication*: same actions or experiments will have similar results and outcomes, every time.
4. *Extrapolation*: what worked in the past will continue to work in the future, with similar intensity and outcome. Thus if you know a little about a system, you can generalize about it.

- Emergence

In conventional strategic planning an organization is viewed as the sum of its parts — the simple addition of departments, divisions, and people. Organizations, however, are complex systems borne out of the *interactions* of their constituent parts. In such systems/organizations, outcomes are mostly *emergent* rather than predictable.

According to the new science of Emergence, the whole is *not* equal to the sum of its parts, but rather it is the product of their interactions. Thus a system's behavior cannot be predicted based on the behavior of its parts. Similarly, emergent behavior is often counter-intuitive and unexpected. "Better before worse" and "worse before better" are two such patterns of behavior of complex adaptive systems.

Better before worse interventions are those that show initial success, but then fail to such an extent that the organization is left worse off than before. Some lauded and hyped mergers and acquisitions were initially applauded, but ended up as a financial disaster for the company (e.g., the Sony–Columbia merger in 1989 resulted in a $2.7 billion write off; the AOL–Time Warner merger in 2000 resulted in a $200 billion loss in stock value and a $54 billion write-down in assets).[5]

Worse before better situations, in contrast, show initial setbacks in performance, but then show improvements with time to higher levels of performance. Most quality management and business process re-engineering (BPR) initiatives fall into this category because the radical change is initially so disruptive, but is eventually more efficient. As decision makers tend to focus on short-term results, they get puzzled and frustrated by these patterns and often over-react or intervene prematurely to the detriment of their organizations.

• Data and Outputs

The common approach to planning is "predict and plan". Strategic plans generally rely on historical data to project and predict future trends. Hence, planning goals are set based on past data extrapolated into the future. Often, ambitious goals are set over a long horizon with much expectation. However, long planning horizons betray forecasts and actual results fall short of expectations.

Organizations also focus mostly on the *output* of planning, namely the document that is "the plan". Hence, considerable time and resources are

---

[5] Ackoff, R. (2006) "Why few organisations adopt Systems Thinking." *Systems Research and Behavioral Science*, 23(5), 705–708.

spent to make sure the document is as detailed and all-encompassing as possible. Thus, most plans end up with an exhaustive "wish list" of desired outputs (deliverables) and outcomes. Often under time pressure, far less time and consideration is given to the buy-in and implementation aspects of the plan. This is the Achilles' heel of planning, a situation in which the involvement and participation of diverse stakeholders make the difference between an elaborate "paper" plan and one that is accepted and embraced rationally and emotionally by those who need to implement it and those who are affected by it. After all, no matter how elaborate or sophisticated a plan is, it is a mere document.

Chapter 3

The Language of Systems Thinking

3.1 Relationships

We recognize symbols such as A, B, C, and D as letters of the English alphabet. These "symbols" have no meaning by themselves in isolation. However, with creativity and proficiency, masterful writers and speakers convert these 'symbols' into inspiring stories and stirring speeches that convey human sentiments of love, hate, anger, laughter, courage, and action. Jesus, Shakespeare, Gandhi, Martin Luther King, and Hitler used language to unleash emotions and stir actions for both good and evil.

Despite the versatility and power of language, none of its constituent elements (letters) has any meaning or value on its own. Thus, the power of the language is realized in the creative *relationship* of its component parts: letters and words. The same is true of music. The sound of a piano or violin produced by a novice can be torturous. Yet the same notes in the hands of Mozart or Vivaldi uplift our souls. Like language, the power and beauty of music comes from the *relationship* of its constituent notes.

To create meaning and beauty words need to be connected. In most languages one cannot explain a word by itself — you need other words to explain any given word. Try to explain "motivation" without using any other word. When words are connected, new patterns emerge that extend the meaning of the individual words beyond themselves. "Motivation" and "effort", for example, when considered separately and in isolation, represent abstract concepts at best — they convey no meaning or context, nor they can explain any interrelated pattern. (More will be said about this shortly.)

The basic "alphabets" (building blocks) of the Systems Thinking language are called variables. Variables are drivers or factors that dynamically determine the behavior of a system. Variables can be concepts, actions, conditions or policies such as quality, working hard, stress, marketing expenditure, company image, sales, revenue, and GDP. One of the key skills of Systems Thinking is to unravel interconnectedness and identify patterns between relationships. Systems Thinking language inculcates this skill for individuals as well as for groups.

Relationships are the underlying cause of complexity. The more interdependent the elements of a system, the more complex the system, and the more unpredictable the behavior of the system. This is known as *dynamic complexity*, which is distinct from detailed complexity which is caused by the sheer number of elements present in a system (e.g., number of investors in the share market, number of parts in an aircraft). Unraveling and understanding relationships is the core of Systems Thinking. Systems Thinking language explains dynamic complexity by unraveling relationships amongst the components of the system.

Consider motivation and effort again. What is the relationship between these words (variables)? Well, one can think about different explanations or "theories". For example one could argue that motivation triggers or prompts effort. While this statement may not be universally true it is a plausible explanation or "theory". Using the Systems Thinking conventions (explained in the next section) we can show this relationship as:

Motivation ──────────────➤ Effort

The link shown by the arrow implies a *causal* relationship between motivation and effort, asserting that motivation *causes* or *affects* effort. This convention can be used to express all causal relationships between and amongst variables of all kind. Here are some examples.

Marking expenditure ──────────➤ Sales

Product quality ──────────➤ Customer satisfaction

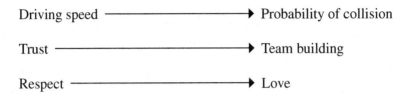

Causal relationships are "statements" — they can express scientific facts, common knowledge, a hypothesis, or one's experience and belief (mental models). The relationships need not hold true indefinitely over time, however.[1]

The basic building blocks of the Systems Thinking language can be extended to create sentences and stories. This means going from one-to-one relationships to forming Causal Loop Diagrams or CLDs — a term used to describe systems models.

3.2 Causal Loop Mapping

Means and End are convertible terms in my philosophy of life.

Martin L. King

Life is underpinned by dynamic forces that constantly change, mostly invisible to us. Back in the 15th century Da Vinci acknowledged that "movement is the cause of all life" (*Il moto e causa d'ogni vita*). Nothing is fixed or stable as the world is in a constant state of motion and flux. Stability is the illusion of a frozen moment of time. In the dynamic *system* of life, all things interact and influence everything else.

Both in nature and society, biological life and societal progress depend on mutual exchange and reciprocity — the immutable law of interdependence. "What goes around, comes around" has been recognized as an indisputable truth by our ancestors. The belief in mutual causality, interdependence, and cooperation as key ingredients of life has been part

---

[1] In reality, the law of diminishing returns applies to most relationships where the direction and magnitude of change can reverse over time.

of all spiritual beliefs and cultures for centuries, especially in indigenous societies.

A Causal Loop Diagram (CLD) is a simple and elegant way of capturing all kinds of intrinsic relationships within systems. One can think of a CLD as a language for describing a system and its internal relationships. These relationships are often hidden and obscure, even to those directly impacted by the interactions. In the words of Peter Senge, CLDs "provide a framework for seeing interrelationships rather than things, for seeing patterns of change rather than static snapshots".[2]

One can tell any story using a causal loop diagram. This can be the story and consequences of a simple act such as smiling at or offering some kindness to someone, or the complex story of how a business venture succeeded or a government policy failed.

As discussed earlier, CLDs are constructed using two "building blocks", namely, variables and links. Variables are drivers or factors that dynamically determine the behavior of a system. Links or arrows simply show the connections between variables. As mentioned earlier, variables can be concepts, decisions, actions, conditions, policies or the state of something that can be measurable (quantitative) like assets, cash flow, sales, staff size, GDP or stock of fish; or qualitative (soft) like reputation, quality, trust, fear, stress, morale, and burnout. In constructing CLDs one can mix quantitative and soft variables together. In fact, the real power and realism of a CLD is its ability to explicitly consider and incorporate soft variables into modeling real world systems.

A model is a representation of a real world system, constructed so that we can better understand the system. "Model" here refers to a CLD and the development of a CLD can be considered a modeling process. Identifying relevant variables is the easier part of the modeling process (see next section). Connecting the variables in a meaningful way is the more challenging part.

Like writing a story, modeling requires creativity and some proficiency of the language. Similarly, there is no one "best" way for the

---

[2] Senge, P., (1990) *The Fifth Discipline — The Art and Practice of the Learning Organisations*, Doubleday Currency, p.68.

modeling process. When creating a systems model, keep in mind that the goal of modeling is to tell a story, the story that emerges from connecting the interacting parts. If the story is sound and logical (i.e., it makes sense and *feels* right) then you have an "acceptable" model. It usually takes three to four iterations of creative drafting to get an acceptable model. Also keep in mind that no model or CLD is *complete* or *perfect* as all models are abstractions of reality or reflections of one's mental model. Ultimately, the *process* of building a systems model (i.e., constructing a CLD) is the most value-add part of modeling as it engenders deep and rare conversations within a group and inconspicuously surfaces participants' mental models.

3.3 How to Identify Variables

"How do I identify variables?" is a question often asked in systems workshops and seminars. Normally managers and decision makers have an issue or problem in mind. The first step is to convert the issue at hand into a "systems question". For example, the issue could be "we have stagnant productivity in our organization". The systems question for this issue would be "What are the factors that affect productivity at our organization?" The answer to this question will unravel key variables for a systems model. Invariably, a workshop setting is an effective and efficient way to solicit this information from diverse stakeholders.

The diversity of the participants could bring to surface contentious points of views and divergent mental models. However challenging though, with appropriate facilitation, the diversity of views will enhance the quality of conversation and the richness of final outcomes. This is an important element in creating consensus decisions and cross-function and cross-sector collaborations. In group settings, all stakeholders must participate in generating variables through brainstorming and discussion. A highly efficient and fun method for "silent" group brainstorming is the Affinity Method, which is described in more detail later in this book.[3]

---

[3] Maani K. and Cavana R. (2007) *Systems Thinking System Dynamics – Managing Change and Complexity*, Pearson Education, Prentice Hall, 2nd edition.

3.3.1 *Tips for selecting variable names*

In building a CLD, variables characterize semantic data. Hence, correct and precise variable names are the key to a meaningful and useful CLD. Additionally, using precise variable names facilitates construction of a CLD and enhances the accuracy of the model. Remember that a variable should be capable of increase or decrease — variables should be able to be attributed with "more" or "less". For example, "state of mind" is ambiguous and cannot increase or decrease, but "happiness", "sadness", and "fear" are specific and can go up or down. In summary, choose variable names that are unambiguous, specific, and precise. In general, around 10-15 variables are sufficient to create a detailed and meaningful systems model. It is important to note that more variables do not make better models. The quality of a model is a function of the *insights* it generates, not the size of the model.

Here are some tips for selecting appropriate names for variables:

• Use nouns rather than verbs for variable names. For example, use "production" rather than "producing".
• Do not include adjectives such as "increased", "decreased", "more", "less", "lower", and "higher" in the variable names. These are captured by link polarities (+) and (−), as explained in the next section.
• Do not use a variable name more than once in any model.
• In most cases it is preferred to use the positive sense of a variable. For example, "encouragement", rather than "discouragement" and "investment" rather than "divestment".

Table 3.2 shows some examples of poor versus good variable names.

Table **3.2.** Examples of poor versus good variable names.

Poor variable names	Good variable names
Environmental effect	Environmental damage (or benefit)
Economy	Economic activity, economic viability, GDP, *etc.*
Consumer behavior	Consumption, spending
State of mind	Happiness, confusion, *etc.*
Cost	Variable cost, fixed cost, material cost, compliance cost
Quality	Process quality, product quality, service quality, *etc.*

3.4 Constructing a Causal Loop Diagram

Creating a Causal Loop Diagram is as much an art as it a science. On average, it takes three to four iterations for a sound systems model to emerge from the chaos of the variables. The end result should tell a coherent and meaningful story, conveying a message with insights.

To begin a CLD, start with the variables that have the most obvious relationships; then add new variables one by one to complete the "story". Remember the logic of each link should be clear and justifiable (i.e., supported by scientific or historical facts/evidence, expert opinion, or even personal experience and judgment). For example, linking "employment rate" to "productivity" in a national economy is not intuitively obvious unless it is supported by economic data or historical patterns. Following these steps can help with this process:

- Start with pairs of variables with *direct*, clear, and undisputable causal connections. For example: cost and profit, punishment and fear, overeating and indigestion, and CO_2 in the atmosphere and Earth's temperature.
- When all directly connected variables have been identified and connected, then complete the story by asking for each variable: "What else is this variable *directly* affecting or being *directly* affected by?"
- Continue with this process until all variables are connected and accounted for.

3.4.1 *Clustering variables*

If a CLD has more than 10 variables, it becomes difficult to construct a coherent causal story including all the variables. In such cases, start by clustering the variables into smaller sub-groups. This should be fairly simple and quick. Examples of sub-groups would be: people or employees, budget or finance, structure or organization, culture and leadership or strategy; or more macro groups such as the environment, economy, policy, and regulations.

Once sub-groups are identified, it becomes much easier to construct a smaller CLD for each sub-group (sub-system). At this stage the link between sub-systems (small CLDs) becomes rather apparent and connecting the sub-systems together will provide an overall CLD or systems model.

It is important to note that not all variables can be logically or conceptually connected. Do not try to connect such variables (and even those with weak logic) arbitrarily for the sake of completeness. In cases where no compelling connection can be found with other variables, a variable can be left alone. This is called a "lone wolf" variable.

3.4.2 *Adding bells and whistles*

Once an acceptable CLD is constructed, the next step is to add link polarities. Link polarities indicate the nature or type of relationship between variables. They are decided upon based on the *direction of change* between pairs of variables, independent of the surrounding links and polarities. For example, assuming normal price elasticity, the link between "price" and "demand" is negative '-' , regardless of adjacent connections, for example demand and supply. Feedback loop types can be identified for each *closed* loop using the polarities or the tracing method (loop types and link polarities are discussed in more detail later).

For clarity and readability, it is a good practice to identify each loop by an appropriate label that reflects an issue or a dimension of the story, such as "economic", "environment", "population", "policy", and "leadership".

Open loops

It is not necessary or desirable that all causal chains form a closed loop. Generally, when external (exogenous) variables are present in the model (e.g., government policy or laws, inflation, exchange rate, natural disasters) in organizational settings, the internal variables within the system cannot influence the external variables, at least not in the short term. For example, laws and government policies affect all citizens, but citizens cannot influence government policies immediately, or at all, depending on how democratic the government is. This influence, though, could happen after long time gaps, through political elections, public pressures, referenda or political or military coups. This point is illustrated in the CLD in Figure 3.2.

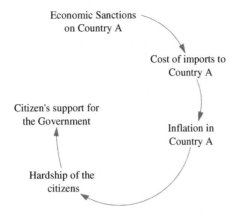

Figure 3.2. Example of an open loop.

Overall, a good CLD is one that is self-explanatory. In other words, the CLD should be of enough clarity that it would not require additional narratives or verbal explanations. At the same time, a good CLD is not necessarily a busy or the most comprehensive one. That is, a CLD does not have to include every possible aspect of the problem or all of the variables that could be thought of. Including only the most relevant or influential variables adds insights or precision to the model.

Most importantly, remember that a CLD is not an *end* in and of itself. A good or great CLD is one that leads to new insights and helps create consensus and shared understanding of an issue or a problem and results in collective ownership and commitment to action by the stakeholders. This is an ambitious goal and has a huge outcome if one can achieve it!

3.4.3 *Link polarity*

In general, an arrow indicates whether and how a variable affects, influences, impacts, or causes changes to another variable. This influence or change can be 'positive' (increase) or 'negative' (decrease). This is indicated by a '+' or '−' sign at the head of the arrow, denoting the nature of the relationship between the two variables.

Figure 3.3. A loop with link polarity.

For example, marketing is expected to increase (+) sales and this produces higher (+) profits. Marketing expenditures also increase (+) cost and lower (−) profits. These "statements" can be shown in the CLD model in Figure 3.3.

Thus, '+' means the two variables move up and down together in the same direction, while '−' indicates the two variables move or change in opposite directions. This is known as *polarity* between two variables. In some cases a causal relationship is not a known or established fact. In such cases one should note these as an assumption, hypothesis, conjecture or even belief.

Link polarity can change over time or within a different range of a variable. The law of diminishing returns (economics) and market saturation (marketing) are examples of change of polarity between variables over time, such as advertising and sales, investment and return, and hard work and productivity.

3.4.4 *Exercises*

At this point in the book, you, the reader, should have enough understanding of causal loop diagrams, variables, and link polarity to construct simple CLDs. The following exercises are intended to test your understanding, model answers follow.

For each exercise, construct a CLD with the variables listed (do not add any other variables) and show link polarities.

Exercise 1
Motivation, effort, performance

<u>Exercise 2</u>
Supply, demand, price

<u>Exercise 3</u>
Population, birth, death

Model answers are shown below.

(a) Case 1 model answer

This was a simple CLD with singular polarities (all positive).

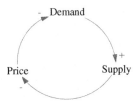

(b) Case 2 model answer

This was another simple CLD, but this time with both positive and negative polarities and the variables were listed out of order as placed in the CLD.

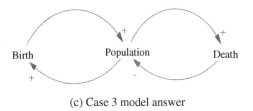

(c) Case 3 model answer

This was an advanced double loop CLD that probably stretched your understanding of how to construct a CLD.

As a further exercise, explain the polarities in the above models in words. A simple way to do this — check the logic of your CLD story — is to imagine explaining it to a five-year old.

3.4.5 An extended example: The dynamics of city growth[4]

The following example captures the dynamics of a city's economy. This is a more complex story as it involves several interrelated variables that collectively depict the dynamics of growth (or decline) of a city's economy. The key variables are:

- City infrastructure and amenities
- Quality of life
- Businesses' performance
- Business activities
- Skilled labor
- Well-paid jobs
- Tax levels
- Tax base

The CLD in Figure 3.4 shows the relationships amongst these variables.

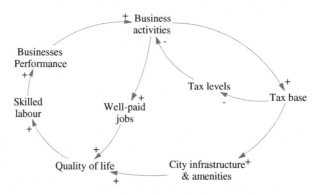

Figure 3.4. City growth dynamics.

---

[4]Adapted from *Business Herald* (2000) New Zealand.

3.5 Feedback Loops

A causal loop represents a *feedback* system. Feedback occurs in two possible forms: *reinforcing* (positive feedback) and *balancing* (negative feedback), the origins of which can be found in science and engineering. Note that here, "positive" and "negative" should not be confused with good and bad — "whether feedback is considered positive or negative depends on what it does to *changes* in the system."[5] The interaction between these feedback forces is the source of complexity in real life.

Feedback processes abound in nature, in society, and in man-made devices. The human body, for example, embodies an amazing array of feedback systems. As an illustration, our eating mechanisms are far more complex than the most sophisticated guided missile. While eating we can move our head and mouth wildly and yet the spoon in our hand rarely misses our mouth. This is because our eating *system* uses hundreds of feedback signals that guide the spoon to our mouth with perfect accuracy. Other biological systems such as breathing, sweating, healing, blinking, blood pressure, body temperature, body balance, hunger, and sleep are further examples of feedback processes. Our "blood alone contains hundreds of chemicals — oxygen, carbon dioxide, water, salts, sugars, enzymes, fats, minerals, hormones, *etc.* — each of which is regulated by one or more loops. Other natural and social systems depend on negative feedback just as much for their survival".[6]

Household appliances contain numerous feedback mechanisms as well. The timing of a toaster, the temperature of a shower, the ballcock in a toilet, and the automatic frequency control on FM radios are but a few examples. In ecology, the relationships between predator and prey, population and disease, and plants and CO_2 balance follow similar feedback cycles.[7]

Feedback mechanisms also abound in business, social, and political systems. Examples are the symbiotic relationships between investment and income, economic recession and corporate income, unemployment

---

[5] Kauffman D. L. Jr. (1980) *Systems 1: An Introduction to Systems Thinking*, The Innovative Learning Series, Future Systems, Inc., p.24.
[6] Ibid, p.12.
[7] Ibid, p.11.

levels and university enrolments, and social justice and violence. At the firm level, feedback patterns are evident in the ripple effects of management decisions and actions on staff motivation and morale, and then on the subsequent performance of the firm.

3.5.1 *Reinforcing feedback*

Reinforcing feedback causes a system to expand — expressed as growth or decline — while balancing feedback resists and dampens change in the system. Examples of reinforcing growth patterns are birth and population, interest earned and bank balance, exercise and health, and encouragement and performance. Reinforcing forces can also lead to continuous decline or downward spiral. In daily language we call this a "vicious cycle", which explains, for example, the relationship between poverty and crime, low investment and business decline, and nagging and withdrawal. Addiction is another case of a reinforcing loop or vicious cycle. Craving for cigarettes, alcohol, and sugar are some examples as the more we consume them, the more we will 'need' to get the same level of satisfaction, creating an escalation or a downward spiral. Reinforcing loops are denoted by the letter "R" inside the loop.

3.5.2 *Balancing feedback*

While reinforcing loops amplify and encourage change, balancing or negative feedback loops negate or dampen change to create stability and control. In other words, they are self-regulating mechanisms. For example, the relationship between birth and population is a reinforcing loop whereas death and population represent a balancing process (refer to earlier population-birth-death CLD).

As suggested earlier, there are numerous balancing mechanisms all around us: in our body, at home, in our workplace, in society, and in nature. Unlike a reinforcing loop, a balancing loop seeks stability, return to control, or aims to reach a goal or target. For example, a company's budgeting exercise (i.e., balancing income and expenditures) represents a 'return to control' loop while a thermostat provides a 'goal-seeking' process. Regulations and policies are all designed to act as balancing feedback; such as law enforcement is to deter crime, social welfare is to reduce poverty, and emissions taxes are to slow down global warming. Balancing loops are also referred to as counteracting or negative feedback loops and are denoted by the letter "B" inside the loop.

3.5.3 *How to identify loop type*

Correct identification of feedback is critical for understanding systems behavior and its implications for decision making. While there are 'formal' methods to identify loop types, with practice and experience feedback loops can be recognized intuitively. Following the 'story' of the loop and its overall effect is one way to do this. For example, in the CLD in Figure 3.5, as interest accumulates it increases the saving balance, and as the saving balance grows it attracts more interest income, and so on. This is clearly a self-reinforcing process that grows larger and larger over time.

In contrast, in the CLD in Figure 3.6, the behavior of the loop is balancing as withdrawals *reduce* the saving balance, which counteracts further growth interest income. In this example, the '+' link between savings balance and withdrawals is assumed, indicating the scenario that more saving increases the propensity of spending. Of course, the opposite case could also be true where more savings makes one more 'stingy' or frugal.

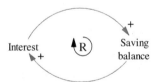

Figure 3.5.   Example of a reinforcing loop.

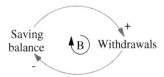

Figure 3.6.   Example of a balancing loop.

3.5.3.1 *A shortcut method*

There is a quick method for telling the B from the R.[8] Count the number of '−' signs (negative polarities) around the loop. If there are no '−'s in the loop or if their total number is *even* (2,4,6....), then the loop is reinforcing. If, on the other hand, the total number of '−'s is odd (1,3,5....), then the loop is balancing. While it sounds simple and fast, the pitfall in this method is that if there are any mislabeled or missing link polarities in the loop then the result is the wrong loop type, which is a much more serious mistake! So it is advised to use the shortcut method as a double check for the intuitive method, and vice versa. In general, while shortcuts can be useful, they can also be misleading and error prone, especially for novice users.

3.5.3.2 *Exercise*

Consider the city growth model in Figure 3.4 and answer the following questions:

- How many loops are in this model?
- What are the loop types?
- What is the interpretation of these loop types?

Answer:

In this example there are three closed loops in the CLD and all three are reinforcing. Depending on the starting conditions, these loops can either be virtuous or vicious. That is, if things are going well (e.g., a vibrant city with a growing business base and activities) then conditions will improve and get better with time. If, on the other hand, there are unfavorable initial conditions (e.g., a deteriorating city with declining business activities) these conditions will get worse over time and create a downward spiral.

3.6 Generic Systems Models (Archetypes)

Systems archetypes are generic systems patterns or "templates" that can apply to diverse areas and a variety of contexts. Sometimes all or a

---

[8]This method was developed by Michael Goodman of the Innovations Associates, Boston.

part of a CLD could represent a systems archetype. However, not all CLDs or stories lend themselves to systems archetypes. In order to identify an archetype, we need to think of and imagine the system at a higher level — a helicopter view. Once you identify an appropriate archetype, you only need a few high-level variables to sketch it.

3.6.1 *Limit to growth*

The truism that "what goes up must come down" suggests growth is not forever. Generally speaking, growth occurs to a certain point, beyond which it will be constrained or impeded by opposing forces. Economists call this the "law of diminishing returns". In marketing it is known as "saturation", which indicates the point at which the market has reached its limit to grow further. In ecology and natural sciences this limit is known as "carrying capacity" of natural resources. Non-renewable resources such as oil (peak oil), arable land and fresh water all have limited carrying capacity.

In systems language, limit to growth is the result of interactions between a reinforcing loop and one or more balancing loops. The turning point occurs when the balancing loop(s) begins to 'dominate' or overtake the reinforcing loop. The CLD in Figure 3.7 shows that the continuous growth in the savings balance is constrained by withdrawals, which act as the limiting factor for savings growth.

More examples of reinforcing and their corresponding balancing forces are shown in Table 3.3.

Another example of limit to growth is shown below in Figure 3.8, where the reinforcing dynamic of love and trust can be destroyed by dishonesty.

The arrow connecting trust and dishonesty is less intuitive and needs explanation. Sometimes a greater level of trust makes it is easier to commit acts of dishonesty. For example, in a trusting community or group it is easier for an ill-intentioned newcomer to deceive and cheat others.

Figure 3.7. Example of limit to growth.

Table 3.3. Examples of reinforcing and counteracting balancing forces.

Reinforcing	Balancing
Love	Dishonesty, jealousy, infidelity, anger, violence
Power	Oppression, corruption
Joy of wealth	Greed, poverty, drug use, laziness
Success	Complacency, arrogance, disillusionment
Crime	Punishment, education, social justice, economic development
Materialism	Moderation, contentment, spirituality
Dictatorship/Oppression	Resistance, uprising
Share market success	Greed, fear
Effort	Burnout
Nagging	Withdrawal

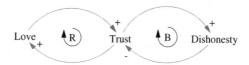

Figure 3.8. Another example of limit to growth.

However, once dishonesty is discovered, trust can quickly turn to mistrust and caution, which help prevent further acts of dishonesty — hence a B loop. Interestingly, an alternative scenario is equally plausible where greater levels of trust could discourage and reduce dishonest acts. In this case the B loop will become an R loop, creating a virtuous reinforcing cycle.

For more practice in constructing limit to growth models, use words in each row of Table 3 to construct CLDs that show the dynamics of reinforcing and balancing loops.

3.6.2 *Quick fix syndrome*

A quick fix is an endemic behavior in society today, rife in business, politics, and personal life. A quick fix has become a cultural habit and accepted practice. We refer to this behavior variously as firefighting,

Band-Aid or stopgap measure, and other analogies. While there is scope and merit in prompt actions and short-term solutions, quick fixes can become counterproductive and damaging if they become a substitute for fundamental and transformative change. More consequentially, quick fixes tend to become addictive, like sugar, heroin, and procrastination. They are addictive because they feel good and they satisfy instantly.

In Systems Thinking this pattern is known as the "Shifting the Burden" archetype, in which one ignores or defers fundamental solutions and interventions in favor of short-term fixes, to the point that one gets terminally trapped (addicted) in this behavior. Shifting the Burden is illustrated in the following story.

In the story, our character is very stressed and tired from workplace challenges and personal relationships. The fastest and easiest way to find relief is go out for a drink at happy hour. This works instantly and makes him/her forget all the pain and trouble — for the moment. The next day, he/she is even more tired and stressed and has a stronger urge to go to happy hour that evening. This is the start of a cycle of dependency and addiction to alcohol.

This story can be shown in the CLD in Figure 3.9. In this CLD, the Shifting the Burden archetype consists of two B loops and one R loop. The B loops represent alternative solutions to the problem of feeling stressed and tired. The happy hour represents a short-term fix, while exercise together with a healthy diet and counselling are long-term fundamental

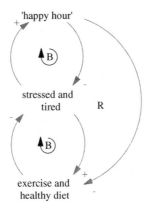

Figure 3.9.   Quick fix syndrome.

solutions. The R loop represents the unintentional consequence of addiction as more use and reliance on the happy hour will weaken the desire and the will for exercise and to eat a healthy diet and to seek professional help.

This is a generic pattern that applies to a wide range of dependency situations and scenarios as a result of excessive use of short-term fixes. Poverty and international aid (handouts), demand for energy and persistent use of fossil fuel, 'bad' behavior and punishment, and declining sales and discounting are some examples of the quick-fix syndrome and the Shifting the Burden archetype.

3.6.2.1 *Mini-case: Good business — bad habits*[9]

Delta-Gamma International makes high-performance, high-quality power tools: chain saws, drill presses, and lathes, primarily targeted at affluent homesteaders and the do-it-yourself market. Since its origins in the 1920s, the company has had a widespread reputation for power and performance. There are actually clubs of Delta-Gamma users, many of whom feel the equipment gives them an aura of being rough-and-tumble loggers.

Like many American industrial firms, Delta-Gamma lost much of its market share to new Japanese competitors in the 1970s. It responded in two ways: first, through a massive licensing effort (producing shop aprons with the Delta-Gamma logo, for instance), which provided enough cash to survive several difficult years; and second, through a company-wide quality improvement drive which made the most of it's limited cash flow.

Delta-Gamma continued to have a terrible problem meeting the demand for its products. At any given moment, the firm had months of backlogged orders. Dealers rarely had enough products to display them in their showrooms.

The backlog stemmed, in part, from a chronic problem with defective equipment, usually found in the last round of testing at the end of the assembly process. Defective products were sent to the "lathe hospital" — a repair shop adjacent to the plant. The hospital had an excellent reputation

---

[9]Adopted from Burson-Benson Case, *The Fifth Discipline Fieldbook: Strategies and Tools for Building a Learning Organization*, 1994.

for fixing defective products, which were then rushed out to customers. It cost almost twice as much to produce a power tool that had gone through the hospital, but everyone knew that without the hospital, the backlog would be much worse.

The company tried to improve its production process to reduce defects on the factory floor, but these improvements were expensive, and the payoffs were slow and uncertain. Engineers could barely make headway in the plant and had more success when they were called in to help solve urgent, complex problems on individual tools at the ever-more-indispensable hospital.

Then another problem emerged. Thanks, in part, to tougher regulatory safety standards for machine equipment, research and development became more expensive and time consuming. A new piece of equipment that used to take six months to develop now took two years. Because of the mystique of the Delta-Gamma image, there was unrelenting pressure to keep introducing new models, but the last four new models were all far behind schedule, and their improvements were all cosmetic — not the performance/design breakthroughs upon which Delta-Gamma rests its reputation.

The charts in Figure 3.10 show the key performance indicators (KPIs) for factory operations over a four-year period.

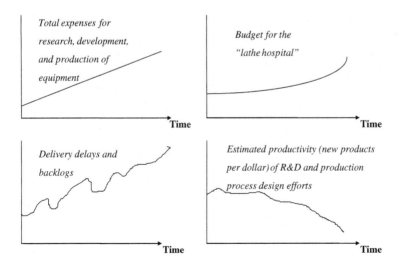

Figure 3.10. Behavior over time graphs for Delta-Gamma.

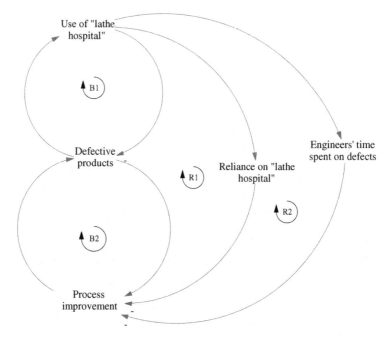

Figure 3.11.   Shifting the burden archetype for Delta-Gamma.

The CLD in Figure 3.11 shows a Shifting the Burden archetype for Delta-Gamma. As the CLD indicates, "defective products" is the main culprit in the story. The company, despite its history and sophistication, is using an old-fashioned and costly approach to deal with defects, namely, the lathe hospital. While this fixes the defects and helps satisfy demand, the unintended consequences of this approach are far more damaging and counterproductive. For one thing, it has created a deep dependency on the lathe hospital and reliance on the engineers to rescue the factory manager, both of which have a detrimental effect on a process improvement initiative, which represents the fundamental solution in this case.

3.6.2.2 *Mini-case: TMP[10]*

This case is set in TMP, a global executive recruitment and consulting firm. The senior managers of the company attended a two-day Systems

---

[10]Adopted from TMP executive course.

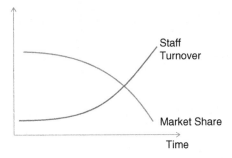

Figure 3.12. Troubling trends at TMP.

Thinking workshop, where they discussed the recent trends troubling their organization. These were a high and increasing staff turnover and a sharp loss of market share, as shown in Figure 3.12. These patterns had persisted and worsened over the last few years.

Normally, organizations view similar 'unrelated' problems in isolation and delegate them to respective functional managers. As in society, it is uncommon for organizations to seek (causal) links between seemingly different issues or problems. However, finding causal connections that are not obvious to managers and decision makers is the cornerstone of Systems Thinking.

In this case, TMP executives, having been through the Systems Thinking training, were asked to think about plausible links between staff turnover and the company's market share in a systemic way. Three hours later, they came up with a CLD (shown in Figure 3.13) that explains the dynamics that had given rise to the company's predicament.

As the CLD shows, staff turnover and market share are *not* isolated issues, independent of each other. Rather, they are dynamically linked and cause mutual growth or decline in each other, as well as in other key areas of the company.

Furthermore, causal relationships between the key variables are far from simple or linear. As shown, they form five closed loops, which indicates mutual interdependence and reinforcing dynamics within and amongst the loops.

The CLD further demonstrates the influence of 'soft' variables such as *motivation* and *recognition* on "Staff T/O" (staff turnover) and their

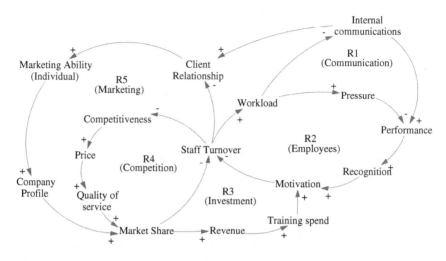

Figure 3.13. Causal loop diagram for TMP.

flow-on effect on other key performance areas such as company competitiveness and client relationships.

Ordinarily, managers and organizations do not engage in Systems Thinking and problem solving principally because managers operate under different and sometimes conflicting KPIs in separate departments or functions (e.g., production and marketing KPI conflicts are well known and widely studied). This fragmentation of functions in silo organizations masks critical links and vital interdependencies amongst functions, departments, and divisions, with adverse effects on the organization as a whole.

Systems Thinking in History

British historian Edward Gibbon studied and documented the history of the Roman Empire in over 20 volumes.[11] Similar to the TPM case, the story of the rise and fall of the Roman Empire can be told by one or more CLDs with several telling reinforcing and balancing loops. The following list summarizes Gibbon's key forces that led to the rise and fall of the Roman Empire.

(Continued)

---

[11]Gibbon E. and Milman H. (2005) *The Decline and Fall of the Roman Empire,* BiblioBazaar.

(Continued)

Reasons for the rise of the Roman Empire:
- Advances in science and technology
- Material resources
- Vast network of roads
- Advanced political/democratic systems
- Motivation to succeed

Reasons for the fall of the Roman Empire:
- Widening gap between rich and poor
- Obsession with sex and low morality
- Love of show and luxury
- Freakishness in the arts masquerading as originality
- Desire to live off the state

3.7 Leverage Points

In daily dialogue, leverage is used to convey small efforts or actions that produce big results, such as "we need to leverage off this investment". Leverage points are especially important in business decisions, corporate strategy, and public policies.[12]

Renowned systems Professor Donella Meadows put this concept in an elegant and powerful definition:[13]

> Leverage points are places within a complex system (a corporation, an economy, a living body, a city, an ecosystem) where a small shift in one thing can produce big changes in everything.

Examples of leverage points are everywhere. A telling example is the economy. As a complex system, the economy comprises and interacts with numerous other systems and subsystems, such as production, supply chain, banking, investments, share market, labor, transportation, the environment, and taxes. The question is: is it really possible for such an enormous

---

[12] For Systems Thinking case studies in policy see Maani and Cavana, *Systems Thinking and Modelling — Understanding Change and Complexity*, Prentice Hall, 2000.

[13] Meadows D. H. (1999), *Leverage Points: Places to Intervene in a Systems*, The Sustainability Institute, p. 1.

system to be 'influenced' by a single variable or index? The answer is yes, and that variable is the interest rate. Tiny movements in the interest rate, even fractions of one percent, can cause big changes in the entire economy and the daily life of its participants. In fact, this is the main intervention that national reserve banks have at their disposal to influence and maneuver the economy through inflation, deflation, or recession. Other examples of leverage are education for eradication of poverty and crime, social justice for a peaceful world, and acupuncture to relieve pain.

A pervasive organizational mindset is that a manager's job is to solve problems. Organizational history and public policy failures show that a focus on narrow and isolated problem solving often results in fixing or removing the problem's symptoms, rather than dealing with underlying causes. Contrary to the prevailing problem-solving culture, Systems Thinking seeks to unravel leverage points through group dialogues and a shared understanding of the drivers of system dynamics. However, as Peter Senge observed, "the areas of highest leverage are often the least obvious. It's the difference between our 'snapshot' views and the deeper, better understanding and mental models."[14] Meadows suggests the two most powerful areas of leverage could be examining "the goals of the system; and the mindset or paradigm underlying the system goals, structure, and rules."[15] However, governments and organizations routinely circumvent or resist delving into these areas due to 'time pressure' and pandering to a voter's whims. In Senge's words, "the higher the leverage point, the more the system will resist changing it."[16] As a result, the endemic obsession with short-term results is a serious impediment to systemic and transformational change in organizations and society alike.

In searching for leverage points, 'hidden' assumptions are often a good place to start. Assumptions influence how things are done in organizations as they underpin beliefs and values shared by a group. Organizational assumptions often have historical or structural roots, which may be long

---

[14]Massachusetts Institute of Technology (MIT) Five Day Organisational Learning Course, 1993.

[15]Meadows D. H. (1999), *Leverage Points: Places to Intervene in a Systems*, The Sustainability Institute, p. 3.

[16]Massachusetts Institute of Technology (MIT) Five Day Organisational Learning Course, 1993.

forgotten by a new generation of staff and managers. Testing assumptions could also unravel hidden feedback loops. For example, a company might believe that financial incentives for 'star' employees will increase the performance of the entire organization. However, this could also create dissatisfaction and jealousy amongst other staff, which would dampen or cancel out the expected benefits of financial incentives — a counteracting/balancing feedback loop.[17]

The George Washington Bridge Story

Opened in 1931, the George Washington Bridge is still the main thoroughfare connecting New York City and New Jersey over the Hudson River via a two-level "double decker" road. One of the busiest bridges in the world, this is the story of how its traffic management team challenged hidden assumptions to solve a long-term and sometimes fatal problem, told by Raymond Gambino.[17]

"In the 1970s, there were many head-on car crashes on the George Washington Bridge causing deaths and severe injuries. Many of these accident victims who required emergency treatment were brought to the Columbia-Presbyterian Medical Center, which was a few blocks from the bridge. At the time little attention was given to see how such accidents could be prevented. Instead, the actors, namely the hospital, police, and the Port Authority, focused on improving their own individual responses to accidents they assumed were inevitable. The hospital was engaged in improving their emergency treatment and measured the effectiveness of its work based on the number of lives saved. The police were busy fining the drivers who crossed the solid yellow lines on the road and measured their success by the number of fines levied. And the Port Authority was busy repainting the yellow lines and it measured the effectiveness of the lines by their degree of visibility to the drivers. Finally, a system redesign was undertaken in order to totally prevent these accidents. As a result, a system change took place: "In the mid-1970s the Port Authority decided to replace the solid yellow painted lines with contoured solid concrete barriers. . . the system redesign led to permanent improvement and zero defects."

The redesign effort concentrated on the reduction of accidents rather than finding a way to better respond to the accidents.

[17]Gambino R. (1990) *Beyond Quality Control*, Lab Report. 12 (5).

3.8 Systems Delays

It is widely recognized that 'delays' or time lags are part of all natural and physical systems — not even the Internet is instantaneous. What is less widely known is that delays critically impact a system's behavior and its reaction to external impulses and change. Delays could be physical or informational and are embedded in all business activities, such as time between placing and receiving an order, need for new staff and hiring, or set-up and change-over times in manufacturing and assembly line operations.

Delays mask and confound cause-and-effect relationships as it is difficult for the human mind to connect short-term events and actions to their long-term and cumulative consequences. This is true because the connections between cause and effect become fuzzy when long delays are present. This is especially pronounced in complex systems, where there are many intervening variables at play between cause and effect.

Examples of systems delays abound. The roots of the 2008 global financial crisis (GFC) are attributed to Ronald Regan's drastic deregulation of financial policies some 25 years earlier. IBM's demise as the unassailable leader in computer and information technology can be traced back to the departure of its visionary founder Thomas J. Watson Sr. some 20 years earlier.

In personal lives, delays between actions and results are prevalent and often with adverse effects: over-eating and weight gain, smoking and cancer, 'small' arguments and relationship break-ups, belittling children and loss of their self-confidence, self-image and one's success or failure in life, and others. Over-eating and weight gain is a good example. Hypothetically, if we could experience in real time how our body weight changes as we eat, we would be less likely to over-eat and there would be fewer overweight people. Although we *know* over-eating causes weight gain, the time lapse before we notice the effect masks their connection. Delays can be equally harmful and deceptive in organizational and political arenas as the outcomes of policies and strategies unfold much later than decision makers anticipate and often with unintended consequences. Thus, lack of awareness and attention to system delays causes organizations and policy makers to make flawed decisions and to create damaging and counterproductive interventions.

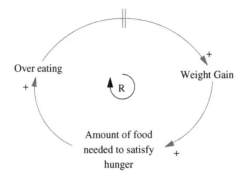

Figure 3.14. Effect of delay in over-eating and weight gain dynamics.

In Systems Thinking, significant delays are identified in the modeling process by the '‖' symbol (parallel bars) on the arrow (Figure 3.14). The effect of delay is especially powerful in balancing loops as it causes oscillations and slows a system's ability to reach stability or achieve its goal.

In System Dynamics — the discipline underpinning Systems Thinking which was developed at the Massachusetts Institute of Technology (MIT) by Professor Jay Forrester in the 1950s — delays can be quantified and can be varied numerically to perform 'what if' analyses to check a system's behavior and sensitivity to variations in delays.

3.9 Behavior Over Time (BOT) Graphs

A Behavior over Time graph (BOT graph) is a simple visual tool that shows changes and variations of a variable over time, normally over months or years. When several key variables are plotted together over time, a BOT graph can provide valuable insights into their relationships and reveal what type of feedback loop drives their behavior. Additionally, one does not necessarily need numerical or historical data to plot a BOT graph. Often, a rough sketch is acceptable and valid, if provided by an expert, manager or someone familiar with the system. A BOT graph is quick and easy to chart, yet it provides a useful tool and valuable insights for managers and decision makers. The demise of Easter Island can be used as an example case to illustrate a BOT graph.

3.9.1 *The demise of Easter Island*

Easter Island is the southeastern most island in the Pacific Ocean, famous for its colossal statues, called Moai. Polynesians settled on Easter Island in the first millennium and created a thriving culture. However, human activity, overpopulation, and gradual deforestation and extinction of natural resources caused the ultimate demise of this civilization. By the time Europeans arrived in 1722, the island's population had dropped to 2,000–3,000, from a high of approximately 15,000 just a century earlier.[18]

Between 400–1600 AD, the Easter Island population was growing steadily, before it began to drop. "In just a few centuries, the people of Easter Island wiped out their forest, drove their plants and animals to extinction, and saw their prosperous society spiral into chaos and cannibalism."[19]

Figure 3.15(a) shows the population pattern of Easter Island from 400–2000 AD. This graph, by itself, cannot reveal the full story behind the population demise. In fact, in problem solving, focusing on a single variable can be misleading as the answer lies in connections between influential variables that cannot be readily 'seen'. In Figure 3.15(b) the pattern of tree cutting activities by the Islanders is superimposed on the population graph. This provides deeper insights into the population decline. As shown in this Figure, the Island's population was growing steadily as long as there was an abundant stock of trees. To support the growing population, tree cutting activities intensified to around 1200 AD when the tree stocks began to decline sharply. Despite this, the population continued to grow until it peaked just before 1600 AD. By then, the stock of trees on the Island had been essentially wiped out and the population began to decline sharply, which led to the demise of the Eastern Island community.

What is the curious lesson here? Why did the people and their leaders allow the exploitation of natural resources to continue for such a long period without any intervention? The obvious answer is that they could not 'see' the link between the vitality of their natural resources and the

---

[18] http://en.wikipedia.org/wiki/Easter_Island.

[19] Fisher, D. (2011) *Modeling Dynamic Systems: Lessons for a First Course*, isee Systems.

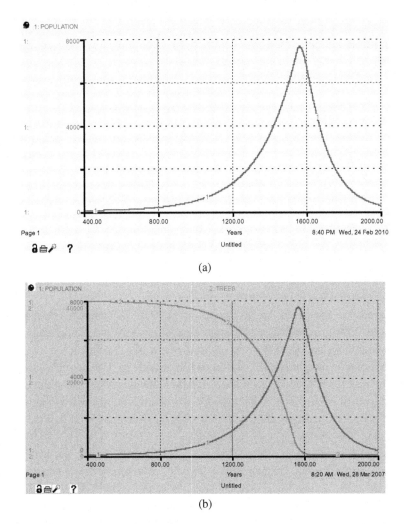

(a)

(b)

Figure 3.15. Simulated Behavior over Time graphs for Easter Island population demise.

preservation of their population. Furthermore, the very long delay between tree felling and population loss masked the link between the two variables.

Ironically, this behavior is happening in today's organizations and societies as *different* and seemingly unrelated problems are viewed and managed by different groups and experts in isolation, each charged with solving a *piece* of the problem. Thus, the inherent interdependencies amongst these problems are not understood, which leaves the *real* problem unsolved. This is prevalent across political, economic, social, religious, and cultural spheres. Are we destined to encounter the fate of Easter Islanders?

3.9.2 Mini-case exercise: A vicious circle of job losses

For the following story, create a CLD that shows the vicious circle mentioned in the case.[20]

Vicious circle of job losses holds up US recovery

While much attention has been paid to the rising number of US job cuts this year, mounting job losses beyond the US are a growing threat to the country's growth, say economists and Federal Reserve officials.

As the economy has slowed, so has Americans' demand for imported goods, and that is hurting growth in other countries.

A drop in exports to the US caused the Mexican Government last month to cut its 2001 growth forecast by almost half — to between 2.5 per cent and 3 per cent this year, down from an earlier forecast of 4.5 per cent.

Mexican "maquiladoras", or factories owned by US companies and located near the border, have cut about 150,000 jobs since the start of the year. What worries economists is that now those workers, in turn, will not be able to afford goods made in the US. It is a *vicious circle* that could delay a US rebound.

Exports to Mexico, the country's second biggest trading partner, fell 5.2 per cent in March. Economists surveyed by Bloomberg News expect the total US trade deficit for goods and services to fall to US$31 billion, from US$31.2 billion in March.

"We're finding out just how integrated global economies have become over the past four to six years," said David Littman, chief economist with Comerica Bank in Detroit. "The wealthier the country, the more a slowdown in income deprives their trading partners of exports. It's a chief aggravating facet of continuing US weakness."

(Continued)

---

[20] Bloomberg article (2000), "Vicious circle of job losses holds up US recovery", 55.

(Continued)

Other trading partners are showing signs of slowing as well, and this has drawn the attention of top monetary policymakers. "The rest of the world, including our key trading partners, is slowing, in large part because US demand was driving foreign growth as well as our own," said Cathy Minehan, president of the Federal Reserve Bank of Boston.

Imports to the US soared when the world's largest economy was expanding at a better than 4 per cent annual rate between 1997 and 2000. But in February and March, the year-on-year increase in imports fell by about 75 per cent as US growth stalled.

Annualized growth in the US over the past six months was just 1.4 per cent, the slowest since the end of the last recession in the early 1990s.

US imports from some other regions have declined in recent months for the first time in years. For example, goods and services coming in from South and Central America dropped in February. The last monthly drop for the region was in January 1999. Imports from Western Europe declined for the first time since June 1996. So far, electronics and other technology-related goods have borne the brunt of the declines, economists said. Weaker demand for Motorola's cell phones, for example, has implications that spread from Taiwan to Mexico.

Advanced Semiconductor Engineering, the second-biggest packager of microchips and supplier to Motorola, says it will report a loss in its second quarter because demand fell more than expected in April and May. The Taiwan-based company is reducing capital spending and cutting pay for top managers.

Motorola has announced plans to cut 600 jobs at a plant in Mexico.

The CLD shown in Figure 3.16 depicts the vicious circle narrated in the above story.

The key insight that can be gained from this CLD is the interdependency of the US and Mexican economies. This interdependency plays out as a vicious cycle pushing both economies into a downward spiral. Breaking this vicious cycle requires long-term collaborative planning and systemic policies to safeguard the welfare of both trading partners and their citizens.

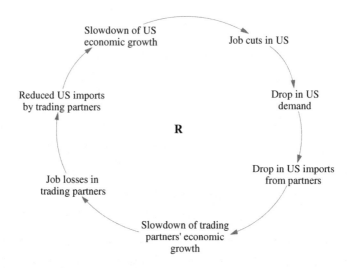

Figure 3.16. The vicious circle of US job losses.

Now that we have seen both the narrative and the CLD depiction of the story, what is the difference between them? What insights can we draw from the CLD model? As the saying goes, "a picture is worth a thousand words". The CLD visually shows the causal relationships and surfaces key patterns out of trivial data and details. Hence the CLD provides a high-level picture of the story.

While analysis relies on numeric data that convey the magnitudes of change ('how much'), a CLD portrays the nature and dynamics of change ('how'), which cannot be readily or easily gleaned from text. In contrast to analysis, Systems Thinking is about *synthesis* or the big picture view.

In many group decision-making situations, agreeing on "the *real* problem" poses the greatest challenge to consensus building and commitment to group decisions. In this regard, a key aspect of constructing a CLD is that it enables a group to develop a shared understanding of the issue or problem. The following chapter expands on this process of group decision making using Systems Thinking tools.

Chapter 4

Multi-Stakeholder Decision Making

4.1 Group Decision Making

Group decision making with diverse stakeholders is a complex, dynamic, and sensitive process. In many of these situations, different people are involved at various stages of the process, representing diverse interest groups. Over time, the continued engagement of broad stakeholders usually leads to sustained collaboration and group learning. In group decision-making scenarios, openness to learning is of paramount importance, as no single individual or agency has all the answers. Nor can group members achieve desired outcomes without knowing the different parts of the problem (system) and how they are interlinked. Thus, group learning should be considered an indispensable part and a desired outcome of group decision making.

4.1.1 Decision making as learning

The decision-making process can be viewed as a "Learning Lab"[1] where open 'group think' and a productive engagement process could generate:

- a shared vision,

---

[1] Maani K. and Cavana R. (2007) *Systems Thinking System Dynamics — Managing Change and Complexity*, Pearson Education, Prentice Hall, 2nd edition.

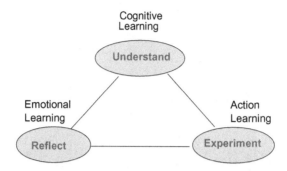

Figure 4.17.   The Learning Cycle.

* common understanding of complexity (i.e., the problem and its drivers), and
* enhanced willingness and propensity for cross-sectorial collaboration.

The Learning Lab is a cutting-edge process for group decision making in complex scenarios. It follows a cyclical process consisting of three inter-linked stages: Understanding (of the problem/system), Experimentation, and Reflection, as shown in Figure 4.17.[2]

The Learning Lab consists of a number of steps and facilitated work-shops. The sessions are generally half- to full-day long. The steps of the Learning Lab are explained after a brief explanation of the importance of shared values in group decision making.

4.1.2 *Group decision making values*

The core values for group decision making must be understood before discussing the four steps of group decision making. It is of paramount importance for the group to genuinely accept and adhere to these values and principles.

* Participation (intellectually and *emotionally*) by all stakeholders
* Respect for all views, peoples, classes, and cultures

---

[2]Ibid.

- Adherence to group decisions
- Suspension of judgment
- Posture of learning
- No fear of mistakes
- 'Us' not 'them'
- No blame

4.2 The Multi-Stakeholder Decision-Making Process

4.2.1 *Before starting — Select the participants*

In order for decision-making outcomes to have power and traction, it is imperative that the decision-making process be inclusive, transparent, and engaging. As a general rule, all key stakeholders should be invited to participate. Depending on the situation, this could include local and central government agencies, businesses, NGOs/community groups, scientists, and other stakeholders. Depending on the relevance and importance of the issue, it may be helpful to invite other interested or influential parties such as selected citizens and the media to sit in as observers. This will help remove any suspicions of secrecy or misreporting of the outcomes.

4.2.2 *Step 1: Understanding and framing the problem*

It is not an exaggeration to say that decision makers often tackle and solve the 'wrong' problem. Surfacing and understanding the 'right' problem within its context — the system within which the problem occurs — is the most critical and often the most neglected stage in problem solving. Understanding complex problems requires differentiating problem symptoms from their multiple and often hidden causes. Hence, the early involvement of stakeholders (e.g., end-users, policy makers, experts) is crucial in unraveling the *real* problem, creating a shared vision and making consensus decisions.

The first step in this multi-stakeholder decision-making process is for the group to articulate the problem briefly and clearly, in one sentence. Defining the problem statement succinctly is not trivial. Most managers, no matter how experienced, find this challenging because complex problems are wicked and have so many facets and dimensions.

As an example, in a workshop with a group of scientists, it took the participants over an hour to agree on a definition of the problem.

There are two reasons as to why defining the problem is so difficult. Firstly, different professionals and knowledge workers use different 'languages' and jargon related to their disciplines. Secondly, and more generally, people have different mental models or mindsets that taint their view of reality and how they perceive the world. This is compounded by the fact that, owing to their training and expertise, most professionals tend to focus on a narrow 'specialist' slice of the problem. This is not surprising as the philosophy and structure of universities and other training institutions are fundamentally disciplinary, focusing on ever narrower specializations. Over the last few decades, in particular, the depth and breadth of subject specializations have proliferated greatly. While beneficial and valuable on many dimensions, this *reductionist* approach to education has come at the expense of a more rounded and holistic education. Consequently, there is a serious shortage of graduates with requisite training and skills for dealing with complex problems facing the world today.

4.2.2.1 *Articulating a rich question*

Articulating a problem or an issue as a question is more powerful than doing so as a statement. A question opens up a problem to more possibilities, rather than pushing it towards closure and a speedy resolution. Commonly, managers embed their 'known' solution into the problem statement. For example: "the problem is we need more staff" or "the problem is we need newer technology". This tendency to jump to a solution hinders open investigation and stifles critical thinking and innovation. Most problem solving investigations start with a "how to" question. The implicit assumption in a "how to" question is that the decision makers already know "what" the problem is. This limits the scope of the investigation to mostly known causes and inhibits a search for deeper root causes. In contrast, Systems Thinking starts with a "what" question to open up a problem to unravel all possible causes and drivers.

Identifying a 'rich question' begins with a group brainstorming on a core issue/problem from different perspectives. This should result in a rich question that is agreed upon by all of the participants. For example, one group might describe a problem as:

Despite huge investments in skills development nationally in the last decade, workplace productivity has not improved.

This is a closed statement that does not lend itself to brainstorming or deep investigation. Additionally, the statement focuses on only two factors, namely, skills and productivity, ignoring other possible variables and drivers that could play a part in this dynamic. For a Systems Thinking exercise, the above statement could be converted to:

What are the drivers/variables that affect workplace productivity?

This question enlarges the problem statement and invites thinking about other influential factors and drivers that provide a systems view of the problem.

4.2.2.2 *Identifying problem drivers*

The next step is to identify drivers and variables that play a key role in generating the problem. This is best done as a *silent* exercise in which each participant, after a period of reflection, *brainstorms* about all possible factors that contribute to the problem. The participants write down a list of drivers *individually* and in silence with no limits imposed. An efficient method to do this is for each participant to write each 'driver' on a separate Post-it note. The significance of individual, silent brainstorming is that it prevents the influence of dominant 'loud mouth' participants and provides an equal voice and 'airtime' for all participants.

Once this step is completed, the participants, working in small groups (4–5 participants each), will combine their drivers into Affinity Diagrams, also known as KJ process.[3] The Affinity Method involves grouping similar ideas/issues/concepts into 8–12 distinct affinity groups or columns. This is not only a very efficient process, most participants

---

[3] Ibid.

also view it as a fun and energizing activity. Maani and Cavana report the following benefits of the Affinity Method.[4]

- Clarifies and synthesizes divergent views using 'non-numerical' data (semantic data)
- Deals with contentious issues in a safe and high-energy environment
- Facilitates formulation of vague and 'messy' problems
- Strengthens teamwork and team spirit
- Creates consensus decisions
- Has the novel element of 'fun', which helps breakdown awkwardness and old baggage.

Table 4.4 is an example of an Affinity Diagram developed by a group of scientists in a workshop in response to the question: What does a transformational change in the plant-based feed supply system of the future look like?[5]

4.2.3 *Step 2: Systems mapping/modeling*

In this step, the variables identified in the problem identification phase are used as *guides* to develop systems models of the problem/issue under consideration. The same groups who created the affinity diagram(s) should continue to collaborate together in this step. While there is no best way to construct a systems model, the following guidelines can facilitate the process:

1. There is no strict rule for building a CLD. Nonetheless, it is important to note that while the variables identified in the previous step may be used in the CLD, they are best viewed as 'thinking guides'. In this regard, individual drivers (single Post-it notes), group labels (header notes), or both may be used as variables. Generally, using individual

---

[4]Ibid.
[5]AgResearch systems workshop, 2010.

Table 4.4. Example of an affinity diagram.

Resilience	High production	Eco-friendly	Economic benefit	Ease of adoption/ system fit	Trees	Lost cost input	Adaptability
• Robust	• Genuine cold weather growth	• Eco-friendly	• It rewards the cost of innovation	• It does not require high conversion costs	• Edible shrubs for hill country with erosion/ drought resistance characteristics	• Nutrient supply = nutrient demand of animal	• Viable formats for differing nutritional needs
• Have the ability to be self — sustaining for 75 years	• Effluent pond grown algae/forage	• Decreases environmental impacts	• People see the value to New Zealand	• Affordable to small as well as large entities	• Edible trees	• Closed system ie, no need for external nutrient inputs	• Hill country forages which only need animal grazing to perform
• Quality = multiple demands	• Hydroponics	• Does not require scarce resources to produce	• Questions of 'why do we need this' have been answered	• It is ethically palatable to interest groups	• Trees	• Plants that re-allocate nutrients to roots prior to harvest	• Self-sustaining non-homogenous pastures for hill country ie, for non-homogenous landscapes
• Multiple benefits		• It doesn't harm other eco-systems	• The benefits to the economy exceed the cost of investment	• Doesn't 'feel' radical — feels obvious		• Minimal inputs → and the inputs which are required are low cost to deliver	• Matching species to landscape

(Continued)

Table 4.4. (*Continued*)

Resilience	High production	Eco-friendly	Economic benefit	Ease of adoption/ system fit	Trees	Lost cost input	Adaptability
• Creates 'usable' by-products		• Riparian strips that are highly productive and remove lots of nutrients from through flow	• Has international partners for more global distribution	• High uptake			• High quality summer producing for low fertility and steep sites
• Extracted protein			• Patent protections during cost recovery	• Applicable to both niche and general farms			• Plants which self adapt to different environments
			• It creates new jobs and sub-industries	• Simple management			• C4s that grow anywhere
			• It is mutually beneficial for farmers and suppliers	• High acceptance			
				• There is infrastructure to support uptake			

drivers would yield a more detailed model whereas using header labels will provide a more abstract and "high-level" model.

2. Sketch Behavior over Time (BOT) graphs (reference models) for the main variables first. This provides a quick visual plot of trends for key variables. This information can be used later to verify the accuracy and consistency of the feedback loops in the CLD. Constructing BOT graphs does not require detailed numerical or historical data, as they are not intended for analysis. As discussed earlier, BOT graphs can be developed using 'mental' data, drawn from stakeholders' experience, and even 'estimates' by knowledgeable participants or experts. This allows a quick construction of BOT graphs, which provides immediate insights into the behavior and dynamics of variables in the model.

3. Identify the feedback loops and their types (i.e., B or R) and check the behavior over time of these loops against the behavior over time patterns identified in step 2.

Once the first-cut CLD models are developed by the small groups, usually after about one hour, they should be shared and discussed within the larger group for the insights, messages, and implications that the models provide.

4.2.4 *Step 3: Identify key leverage points*

As discussed earlier, leverage points are key variables in the system that offer the greatest opportunity for fundamental and sustainable solutions to problems. Generally speaking, there are no quick and easy rules to identify leverage points, as leverage points cannot be derived from conventional quantitative analyses. Instead, discovering leverage points mostly depends on deep discussion and genuine agreement within a group.

In this regard, carefully examining a CLD can identify potential areas of leverage. Additionally, because CLDs provide a shared picture of reality for the participants, this facilities group agreement on the leverage points. Having a group consensus on a leverage point or points is a strong signal for the 'correct' leverage point. This is so as the unity of thought by a group is a powerful foundation for buy-in and commitment to actions. As Meadows points out, shifting one's mental model is far more powerful than the usual interventions in a physical, structural or financial system.[6] This is evident as people's beliefs (e.g., religion, nationalism, racism) are the most powerful drivers of behavior and action.

As a general guide, the following points may be used for the selection of leverage points.

1. Root causes of problems provide for deeper and more powerful leverage areas.
2. Variables with the most connections (i.e., arrows coming in and out) are likely candidates for leverage, as influencing these will have a chain effect on other variables and the system as a whole.

In Part 2 of this book, the Siem Reap (Cambodia) tourism project tells the story of a profound shift of thinking of the officials as the result of identifying a leverage point.

The following Table 4.5 can assist in leverage point selection.

4.2.5 *Step 4: Intervention strategies*

Once leverage points are identified and agreed upon, the final step is to turn them into intervention strategies and actions. Intervention strategies directly address and contribute to leverage points and may include conventional business plans, detailed actions, projects, or programs. There may be several intervention strategies for each leverage point. In order to operationalize intervention strategies, their associated timelines and resources (e.g., people, money, IT), as well as internal and external constraints, need to be identified. Operational measures (i.e., KPIs) should also be checked for internal consistency to avoid or minimize trade-offs. Overall, this process could follow a conventional project management approach.

It is important to emphasize that the aim of *systemic* intervention is changing the *system*, not the symptoms, to bring about discontinuous change and transformation. Thus, systemic interventions are different from conventional solutions and their effects and outcomes may not appear at times and places initially expected.

---

[6]Meadows D. H. (1999), *Leverage Points: Places to Intervene in a Systems*, The Sustainability Institute.

Table 4.5. Leverage point selection guide.

Leverage area	Your influence (D, I, N)	Strategic impact (1–10)	Required effort (resources) (1–10)	Leverage *ratio = impact/ effort	Key stakeholders	Key decision makers	Who leads the change?	Time required to implement	Time to notice change

D = Direct I = Indirect N = None/not significant

*High leverage ratio = Low hanging fruits *Low leverage = Big ticket items

Table 4.6.   Example of intervention strategies based on selected leverage points.

Leverage point[1]	Intervention strategy[2]	Actions/projects/programs[3]	Team/taskforce (leader)	When*	Operational measures**	Soft indicators	Strategic measures	Constraints/barriers***
Staff Morale	1-Staff development	— Institute leadership programs — Create sabbatical leaves		Jan-June 2009	— Programs completed — No. of staff attended — Days of training	— Staff morale — Willingness to participate — Energy levels — Staff socialising — Engagement	— Staff turnover — Productivity — New patents & products	— Budget — Time — Motivation
	2-Participatory planning	— Organise workshop style planning						
	3-Open communications	— Create open feedback system						
	4-Incentive systems	— Investigate team bonus schemes — Survey what motivates staff						
Workload	1-Reduce range of work	— Reduce concurrent projects						
	2-Build up capacity	— Recruit new staff — Encourage teamwork — Train						— New investment

Table 4.6 shows examples of intervention strategies based on two leverage points. As mentioned earlier, leverage points are those areas having the greatest potential for fundamental and sustained change. These are generally factors that influence the system as opposed to fixing the symptoms of the problems. As shown in the table, in addition to the conventional KPIs (operational measures), 'soft indicators' are also explicitly included in the table to complement the 'hard measures'. Soft indicators or 'intangibles' are powerful lead indicators of performance, which can provide managers with the pulse of the organization.

Once this step is completed, it would be enlightening for the participants to compare their original views of the problem and its solutions and the systemic interventions identified through this process. Explaining differences between their original views and mindsets and the learning lab outcomes would be very insightful and educational for the group. These reflections and sharing new perspectives will be an important part of group learning and cohesion.

4.3 Learning Lab for Organizational Cohesion

Extensive research in psychology, management, and economics highlights the shortcomings of the human mind and decision makers' misperceptions of causal relationships and dynamics in complex systems, most notably in feedback, non-linearity, and delay.[7] Research also shows the fallacy of learning from experience, as decision-makers' "perceptions of the system

---

[7]Morecroft, J. (1983) "System Dynamics: Portraying Bounded Rationality." *OMEGA* 11(2).

Sterman, J. (1989) "Modeling managerial behavior: misperceptions of feedback in a dynamic decision making experiment." *Management Science* 35(3).

Sterman, J. D. (2001) "System dynamics modeling: tools for learning in a complex world." *California Management Review*, 43(4).

Senge, P., (1990) *The Fifth Discipline — The Art and Practice of the Learning Organisations*, Doubleday Currency.

Maani K. and Cavana R. (2007) *Systems Thinking System Dynamics — Managing Change and Complexity*, Pearson Education, Prentice Hall, 2nd edition.

Maani, K. and V. Maharaj (2004) "Links Between Systems Thinking and Complex Decision Making." *System Dynamics Review* 20(1).

dynamics are often (if not always) different from the actual performance. Their ability to interpret feedback is critically limited, and even when given multiple opportunities, improvements in decision-makers' performance and awareness are not evident."[8] These findings have critical implications for management education and practice and highlight the need for Systems Thinking training for managers and decision makers.

In the Learning Lab, the participants, through experiential learning and conceptual systems modeling, will seek to understand the interrelationships and dynamics in complex systems — a critical skill which leads to deeper insights for decision makers. In this setting, the systemic problem-solving process challenges participants' mental models and tests hidden assumptions inherent in complex systems. Further, the elements of intellectual challenge, curiosity, and fun create enjoyment and enthusiasm for group learning and teamwork.

In summary, the Learning Lab process enables the participants and their organizations to:

- Understand and deal with ambiguity, uncertainty, and complexity
- Foresee the unintended consequences of decisions, policies, and strategies
- Identify fundamental causes and solutions to chronic problems
- Avoid misjudging problem symptoms for their causes
- Reconcile the dilemma of short-term fixes versus long-term strategies
- Resolve endemic staff morale and productivity problems
- Bring alignment of vision and action to teams, functions, and divisions
- Facilitate finding leverage points for sustainable interventions

Once established, the Learning Lab can serve as a thinking space for group decision making, a place where management strategies and policies can be tested for blind spots and unintended consequences. During the reflection part of the Lab intermediate outcomes, both successes and failures, will be scrutinized and changes and adjustments can be made.

---

[8]Li A. and Maani K. (2011) *Dynamic Decision-Making, Learning and Mental Models*, University of Auckland Working Paper.

Repeated use of the plan-experiment-reflect cycle will lead to new levels of learning and performance over time (i.e., continuous improvements).

4.4 Mini-case: Multi-Stakeholder Decision Making (MSDM)

This mini-case in MSDM tells the abridged story of a problem-solving assignment by a group of scientists and managers affiliated with a national science organization employing over 600 scientists with expertise in a wide range of disciplines. Owing to the great diversity of disciplines in the organization, their tendency was to work in 'silos'. Over the years, the management had encouraged staff to collaborate across disciplines and projects, without much success. This was both frustrating and puzzling to management, as well as the staff. The purpose of this exercise was to understand the reasons for this failure to collaborate.

After initial discussions with management, this question was articulated for the workshop:

What are the barriers and drivers for collaboration at our organization?

To answer this question in a Learning Lab setting, a cross-section of staff with different expertise were invited to participate in the workshop. The participants represented a diverse range of disciplines and organizational roles, as well as a demonstrable interest in the workshop question and its outcomes.

The participants used the Affinity Method, which yielded over two dozen variables. These variables were converted into a CLD, as shown in Figure 4.18. As the CLD shows, there are several factors, relationships and feedback loops beyond any simple intuitive 'solutions'. A typical answer (solution) to lack of collaboration within and across organizations is to have more communication. "We need more meetings" is a familiar expression in these cases. The Learning Lab experience was able to generate more introspective and precise solutions.

In this systems model, all but one of the feedback loops is reinforcing (R). This signifies that if the initial conditions (e.g., organizational culture, attitudes, history) are not favorable, these conditions will get worse with

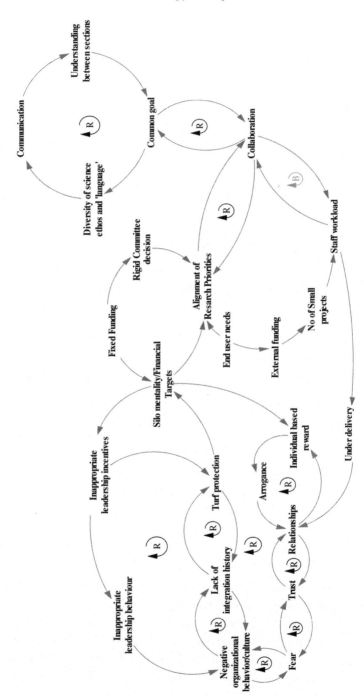

Figure 4.18. CLD showing barriers to collaboration.

time. In other words, these conditions act as vicious cycles, which create inertia and resistance to change that hold the organization down.

In this CLD, a telling feedback loop (in the lower right corner) is the reciprocal relationships between collaboration and workload. When mandating more collaboration, management rarely seriously or explicitly considered the impact on workload. In reality, though, collaboration increases workload, at least initially, as collaboration requires a great deal of communications, reiterations, and coordination. This is a real impediment to collaboration as staff wish to avoid the 'extra' work and get on with their 'own' jobs. In systems language, the relationship between workload and collaboration creates a balancing or self-correcting loop, which dampens and prevents sustained collaborative efforts across organizations and sectors.

4.5 Conclusion

Part 1 of this book established the need for new approaches and appropriate tools for decision making in multi-stakeholder situations. A number of systems thinking tools were presented and examples were used to demonstrate their applications. Part 2 will present seven detailed case studies of real business and policy situations to further reinforce the materials learned in Part 1.

Part 2
Cases

Case 1A

Resolving Conflict in a Supply Chain[1]

Foodcom[2] is a major global food and nutrition company with operations on five continents. This case study was conducted in one of its distribution subsidiaries employing approximately 700 staff. The case highlights deep-seated problems within the supply chain division and how simple applications of Systems Thinking tools helped the staff and the company to resolve endemic conflicts and enable a collaborative culture.

The case demonstrates two scenarios within the supply chain. Each scenario describes four levels of thinking — Events, Patterns, Systemic Structure, and Mental Models[3] — and shows the unintended consequences of management views, assumptions, and decisions and their effects on day-to-day behavior of the staff and the company's performance.

Before discussing these scenarios, it is noteworthy to examine the organization's culture, namely, the attitudes and assumptions that influence behaviors and shape relationships. The following verbatim statements,

---

[1] Cases 1A and 1B are adapted from Annie Fan's MCom thesis *Using System Dynamics to Understand Trade-Offs amongst KPIs*, The University of Auckland, 2007.
[2] Fictitious name for a real multi-national company.
[3] Maani K. and Cavana R. (2007) *Systems Thinking System Dynamics – Managing Change and Complexity*, Pearson Education, Prentice Hall, 2nd edition.

made by the staff representing different functions within the supply chain, reflect this culture *before* the Systems Thinking intervention:

- *It's just not good enough, you guys at the front line need to keep us informed, we can't keep on doing this. We are spending thousands of dollars rushing around in the hope to raise our CFR [case fill rate], but our performance seems to be going down even more.*
  — Supply planner

- *There is no such a thing as oversold — sales have basically under forecast and there is a communication breakdown.*
  — Demand planner

- *We are way off our target CFR of 98% — category A is currently averaging around 70%! I'm constantly getting hammered by unhappy customers about missed orders ... We've got to do something!*
  — Customer services manager

- *What happened this quarter? Our airfreight cost has gone through the roof! In addition, our local delivery charges between North Island and South Island have also increased due to more urgent truck deliveries instead of rail. What's happening in the planning team?*
  — Supply chain financial controller

These statements show an attitude of resentment, blame, finger-pointing, and us-versus-them, which is common in organizations when things go wrong. In contrast, the statements below, which were made *after* the Systems Thinking intervention, demonstrate a stark change of attitude and feelings towards co-workers and their relationships:

- *I never thought about the problem this way, now I see! I guess I was a little selfish... I was probably the one that caused all the chaos in the supply chain. I shall arrange more meetings with supply chain staff to find out more about what they do.*
  — Key account manager

- *It's amazing how I have actually created these problems for myself!*
  — Supply planner

- *I have got more exposure to other parts of the business, especially marketing's view on market share and product ranging... This is*

beneficial; we should get more people involved in similar cross-functional discussions. It could add a lot of value.
— Factory performance manager

So, what happened that caused this change?

Below we discuss two problem scenarios that the company had been grappling with. The staff, under pressure from management, had 'solved' the problems in their own way, but with adverse unintended consequences. To their dismay, their 'common sense' solutions had exacerbated the problems and escalated the cross-functional stress and confrontation, as reflected in their *before* statements.

Scenario One: Why Out-of-Stock Solution Failed?

When enquiring about 'troubling' issues in the supply chain, the staff were quick to point to the chronic out-of-stock (OOS) situation at Foodcom, as evidenced by:

- Goods receipting time had increased from five days turnover to nearly eight days.
- Out-of-stock products had noticeably increased and accelerated.
- Warehouse and distribution staffs frequently complained about the workload and stress.

Managers typically attempt to 'solve' problems as quickly as they appear-invariably treating them as symptoms. This jumping-to-solution tendency circumvents a careful understanding of deeper and connected issues related to the problem. In Systems Thinking, symptoms are treated as 'events' or a shallow snap shot of reality. To gain a richer picture of events, one must examine their pattern over time. For this scenario, Foodcom staff produced the graph in Figure 1 that traces the sequence of OOS events over time.

While this graph provides further insights into the events, it does not explain how and why the OOS situation kept getting worse — despite the best effort of the staff to release products ahead of their planned schedule (devanning).

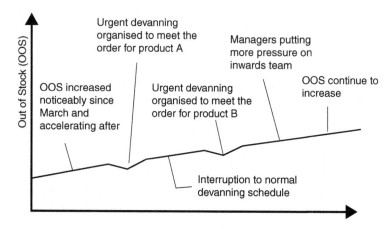

Figure 1.   Events related to out of stock.

At this point the supply chain study group decided to construct a CLD to explain the interconnections amongst these events and related actions. This resulted in the following simple CLD developed by the staff (novice users) with the help of a facilitator.

The CLD in Figure 2 captures the dynamic interplay amongst key variables affecting the OOS situation and the overall performance of the supply chain.

The 'B' loop shows the relationship between the OOS problem and management's intended solution, namely, "urgent devanning". While this solution *worked* as a short-term measure, it led to an interruption to normal devanning, which had two unintended consequences: increased goods receipting time and higher staff workload due to double handling. These, in turn, (a) reduced inventory level and increased OOS, making the original problem worse, and (b) increased staff stress and turnover. These chain effects are shown by the two 'R' loops.

Mental Models (The Why)

While the CLD in Figure 2 reveals the underlying relationships that prompted the behavior of the supply chain, it does not explain the hidden

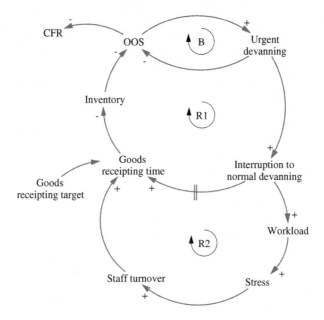

Figure 2. CLD of consequences of urgent devanning.

thoughts and feelings of the players, namely, why they did what they did. To understand this, the most fundamental layer of the puzzle, one must understand the mental model of the decisions makers and players (here, managers and staff).

To this end, staff were interviewed in private and asked to share their thoughts and feelings about the situation. The thought bubbles shown in Figure 3 indicate the unspoken mental models of respective players.

As the bubbles show, the following statements aired during the interviews reflect the unspoken views and feelings of the staff:

- Management team: *Warehouse guys are too slow, we need double shifts.*
- Finance team: *The cost of goods is unacceptably high.*
- Planning team: *We need more urgent devanns.*
- Inwards team: *We will keep our nose down.*

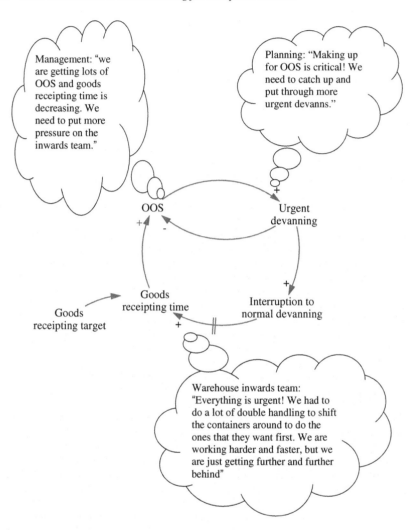

Figure 3.   Thought bubbles of supply chain management and staff.

Follow-Up Study

In order to check whether Systems Thinking intervention had lasting impact on the staff and the company, we revisited the case some 16 months after the initial research and asked three questions:

Q1: Whether collaboration and mutual support between supply chain functions had continued post Systems Thinking intervention?

A: *Yes, particularly in the Supply Chain team. There is a strong consensus amongst the entire SC division that communication and cross-functional collaboration had become the key area of focus for business success.*

Q2: Had initial performance improvements been sustained?
A: *The main SC KPI results (e.g., demand plan accuracy (DPA), CFR, Stock Cover, Bad Goods) have all shown consistent improvement. CFR, for example, reached 97.5% (from 70% before).*

Q3: Whether the employees had continued to utilize Systems Thinking concepts to maintain a culture of continuous improvement and learning?
A: *Since the introduction of Systems Thinking, Foodcom has initiated a "One Number" principle — a holistic view of business where cross functional stakeholders collaborate together and share responsibility to achieve a single company target.*

Further reflection by the staff highlights this change of culture:
Before:

> *The SC team is the whistle blower, because they are usually the one that says NO to marketing's new product launch ideas, NO to the promotion date that we have organized with the trade, they are the one that stops all the fun!"*

After:

> *I never thought about an issue this way, now it seems so simple and it is all common sense. Why didn't we look [at] the situation this way before? I now understand why they [supply chain team] are always challenging our ideas. To be honest we never actually think about whether it is cost effective or whether the inventory level is enough to go ahead with promotion...[before] it wasn't really my problem. My only concern was how we can increase sales from particular activity. I missed the whole idea of the big picture and was only achieving local optimization.*

Using Systems Thinking language, a staff member comments:

> *"I didn't really see how I could help the SC department in terms of reducing bad goods and distribution cost, because, after all, my job is demand planning and concentrating on the DPA (demand plan accuracy) and making sure that we meet our target of 75%. But now, through identifying these causal relationships, I understand!*

He continued his thought process by 'drawing' a causal loop in the air using his fingers:

> *"If the forecasted volume is too high, inventory goes through the roof; cost of working capital increases. Moreover, stocks become aged and will need to be written off when the expiry date hits us. Alternatively, if the forecasted volume is too conservative, we will be out of stock, which hits our CFR. In order to counter attack OOS, we need to arrange urgent devanning, urgent deliveries by truck to SI, which again increases more OOS. The loop just keeps on going!"*

Conclusion

This case demonstrates why and how conventional management of the supply chain at Foodcom — whereby sales set its own target, supply chain forecast another figure, and finance would budget for another number — resulted in endemic dysfunctional behavior. The emerged view shared by management and the staff is that the benefits from using simple Systems Thinking tools with novice users had profound and enduring effects within the organization.

Overall, all of the participants had a positive attitude towards System Thinking concepts. Their level of enthusiasm and engagement in the study demonstrated this. Some participants were keen to do further readings and take formal courses on System Thinking. Overall, the participants agreed that the transformational change in behavior occurred due to developing a shared understanding of the problem across functions and focusing on the big picture. One manager's conclusion was that:

> *The key take-home for me from this discussion session will be regarding understanding of 'working as a whole' concept; that write offs are not SC's [supply chain] responsibility alone. Our sales trade spend budget and SC's write off are really from the same bucket of funding.*

Case 1B

The Dark Side of Product Variety

Another problem that Foodcom had been grappling with was in relation to their product variety (ranging). Product variety is a common marketing strategy companies use to gain market share and increase revenue. In this scenario, Foodcom had recently experienced the following events:

- Product ranging had reached 20 different product lines (five different flavors, each in four configurations).
- Market share was tracking according to plan, and currently Foodcom was the top supplier for this category.
- Factory complexity had increased substantially.
- Cost of product had also increased correspondingly.

The BOT graphs in Figure 4 show these trends.

These patterns indicate a systemic relationship between product variety, factory complexity (production schedule), and product cost. The CLD in Figure 5 was developed by the supply chain staff to show these causal relationships.

The CLD shows the interplay between a reinforcing and a balancing loop. The R loop captures the supporting relationships between product variety, market share, and profit. The B loop, in contrast, shows the unintended consequence of product variety, namely increased factory complexity resulting in higher product cost. This simple picture reveals the side-effect of an otherwise logical and commonplace strategy. In theory,

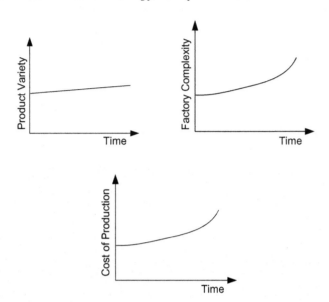

Figure 4.   BOT graphs of product variety patterns.

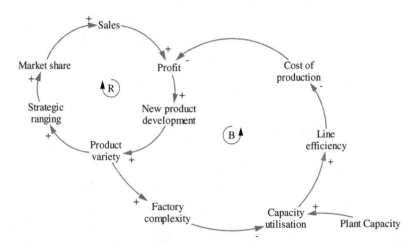

Figure 5.   CLD of consequences of product variety.

an increase in product variety should result in higher sales and profits. Yet in practice, management, motivated by a single-minded pursuit of short-term profits, overlooked unintended consequences, which undermined Foodcom's long-term performance.

This exercise highlighted the blind spot of a commonplace strategy. Following the study, the management team decided to curtail the product range for a more long term and sustained profit margin.

Reflections and Conclusions

The use of Systems Thinking to investigate the consequences of the product variety strategy at Foodcom led to these reflections and conclusions:

- Identification of cause and effects helps unravel how actions today relate to future consequences.
- A focus on causal structures of the problem and "leverage points" increased supply chain performance.
- Organizational performance can be improved if concealed trade-offs amongst KPIs are identified through deeper understanding of their interdependencies from a holistic view of the system.
- Systems Thinking concepts and models enhance team learning and create team commitment.
- Benefits are derived as much from the process of 'thinking together' as the outcomes.

Group Dynamics and Organizational Learning

Post study reflections by the group identified the following lessons from the Systems Thinking exercise:

- Systems Thinking allowed the group to collectively develop and share knowledge and insights.
- Understanding and valuing the big picture prevents sub-optimization.
- Using Systems Thinking captured a holistic view of the KPIs and their interdependencies. It also catalyzed and enhanced team dynamics and organizational learning.
- Giving participants the opportunity to engage in the process of inquiry increased their knowledge of cross-functional dynamics and changed their mindset and behavior.
- The System Thinking exercise created an open environment for cross-functional dialogue and learning with a positive impact on culture and organizational performance.

Case 2

The Pitfalls of Rapid Growth[1]

This case tells the story of Senstech,[2] a hi-tech sensor manufacturing company employing over 400 workers in China with sales offices in Taiwan and the USA.

Senstech produces 200,000 sensors annually, using over 100 types of raw materials assembled mostly by hand. The production schedule is driven by sales forecast and customer orders. Sales and production coordination is conducted weekly, when the production schedule is adjusted based on the latest sales information.

Rapid Growth, Unexpected Consequences

In recent years, the company had experienced a period of rapid growth, but while the management was celebrating success, a host of problems began to surface:

- Production lead time increased from 4 to 6 weeks to nearly 12 weeks.
- Customer complaints rose markedly and, despite high switching costs, many customers cancelled orders and opted for competitors.
- Sales and production department managers and staff were finger-pointing, blaming each other for the problem.

---

[1]This case study was conducted by Kent Koh *et al.* as part of the Helsinki Executive EMBA Systems Thinking course, 2006, Singapore.
[2]Fictitious name for a real company.

- The cost of internal communications sky-rocketed to over $10,000 a month.
- Under pressure, sales people began to leave the company in hordes.
- Despite moving to a three-shift schedule, backlogs remained at record highs.
- Capital tied up in work in progress (WIP) and finished goods (FG) inventories rose significantly.
- Staff started to hide mistakes and tell lies, which led to plummeting morale and deteriorating relationships.

The BOT graphs in Figure 6 show some of the key patterns discussed above.

Causal Loops

The CLDs in this section capture the story of how the rapid growth at Senstech backfired, creating unintended consequences and counterproductive outcomes.

It all starts with the customer

As customer orders increased, production load increased and this led to longer production lead times (B1 loop in Figure 7). Longer lead times caused customer dissatisfaction and triggered many unhappy customers to drop their orders and switch to the competition.

Upset customers, unhappy sales

A mass exodus of customers due to declining customer satisfaction caused increased sales pressure, which led to low staff morale. Depressed morale and high pressures eventuated in the departure of many sales staff from the company. As the sales force depleted, customer orders experienced a further drop. These dynamics are shown in the B2 loop in Figure 7.

When visibility is lost

One of the consequences of lengthy production lead time is that the company loses market visibility. Low market visibility decreases forecast

Sales

10yr   3mon   6mon

Sales were steadily increasing in the first 10 years, followed by 3 months of sharp rise reaching the peak. However, sales took a sharp fall after the peak.

Lead Time

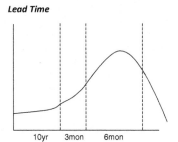

10yr   3mon   6mon

Production lead time was stable around 4-6 weeks over 10 years, before experiencing a sharp increase and dropping quickly due to large customer order cancellations.

Number of Rush Orders

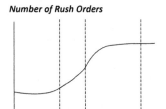

10yr   3mon   6mon

The number of rush orders was almost stable in the first 10 years. However, it rose in the following 3 months and quickly reached and stabilized at a peak.

Number of Cancelled Orders

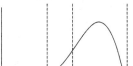
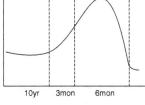

10yr   3mon   6mon

Cancelled orders were relatively stable in the first 10 years. Starting in the following 3 months they sharply rose to a peak. Then, because of decreased sales, the number of cancelled orders dropped quickly.

Staff Morale

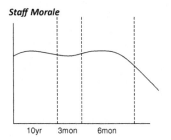

10yr   3mon   6mon

Staff morale was stable in the first 10 years, before it began to decline rapidly in the last 6 months.

Communication Cost

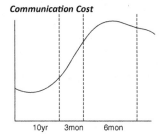

10yr   3mon   6mon

Communication costs also increased sharply and peaked in the last 6 months before decreasing slowly.

Figure 6.   BOT graphs for key variables.

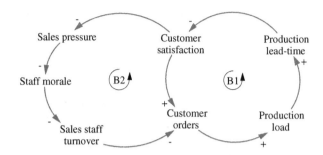

Figure 7. Dynamics of customer orders.

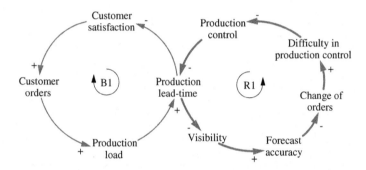

Figure 8. Consequences of lengthy production lead time.

accuracy, which causes frequent order changes that make production control more vulnerable. Production vulnerability extends the lead time further creating a vicious cycle as shown in the R loop in Figure 8.

Another consequence of longer lead time is the slowdown in product release. This, in turn, increases the backlog of production (i.e., work order issuance in Figure 9). The increasing production queue causes further loss of control, adding more time to production lead time. This vicious circle is shown in the highlighted R2 loop in Figure 9.

What about the finance?

The accumulation of orders in the production queue caused by increased lead time creates large work-in-progress inventories (WIP) that tie up sizable capital. This has a severe negative impact on financial performance.

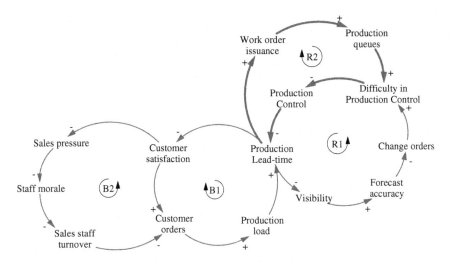

Figure 9. Dynamics of production lead time and production capacity.

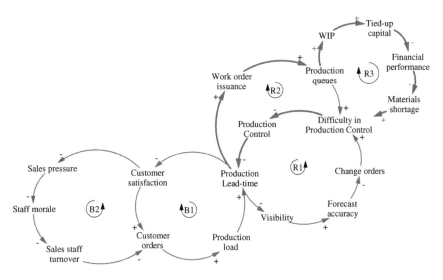

Figure 10. Effect of production lead time on WIP and financial performance.

As a consequence, materials procurement slows down, causing material shortages, which exacerbate production vulnerability and stretch the lead time further — another vicious cycle as shown in the R3 loop in Figure 10.

The rising rate of order changes not only increases the complexity of production control, it also increases the idle stock. The larger the idle

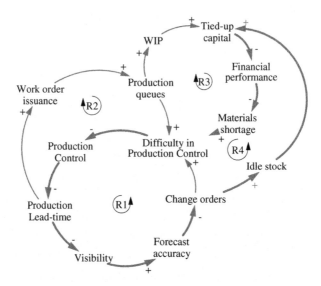

Figure 11.   Production lead time and idle stock dynamics.

stock, the more capital is tied up in inventories and this is another contribution to worsening financial performance. This is shown in loop R4 in Figure 11.

Another hidden consequence is that a longer lead time makes customers unhappy and lowers their satisfaction. Loss of customer orders exacerbates the company's financial performance. This is shown in loop R5 in Figure 12. Hence, the cycle repeats!

Mental Models

The causal loops in Figures 7 to 12 tell the story of *how* Senstech's rapid growth became its worst nightmare. The case study also revealed several fundamental mental models that explain the *why* underlying management's behavior.

Success leads to complacency

When customer orders grew substantially, staff thought that the company was doing quite well. This triggered a widespread sense of complacency,

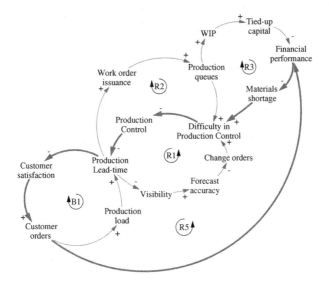

Figure 12. Effect of lead time on firm's financial performance.

which turned out to be quite detrimental. This sense of self-satisfaction lulled the staff to misinterpret the situation to the point that when the number of rush and changed orders were increasing dramatically, they didn't think of it as a big deal.

When production is delayed, issue more orders!

As sales began to decline as a consequence of longer production lead times and decreased customer satisfaction, the sales department increased its effort to win more orders. However, this only increased the production backlog and made the situation much worse, creating a vicious cycle.

When you fear blame, hide your mistakes!

This harmful attitude became widespread within the company, affecting staff behavior and their relationships. Thus, when they felt threatened to be blamed, employees hid their mistakes or pointed fingers at others. Therefore, the real reasons for process mishaps and product defects went unnoticed and consequently wrong 'solutions' were applied, which made the situation much worse.

In conclusion, while the management and staff celebrated the growth of Senstech, in effect their success pushed them into quick fixes and reactive decision making, which caused the demise of the company. They missed the lesson that growth brings not only opportunities, but also risks and challenges. The key to success is to develop organizational capacity to maintain the growth and build on it.

Case 3

Turning Conflict into Consensus

This case study took place in a division of the Ministry of Health in New Zealand. The division employs staff with diverse clinical and policy backgrounds and varying periods of tenure within the organization. As part of their annual business plan, the management was reviewing work priorities for the division. The manager's goal was to *reduce* the division's work areas from around 20 to 6–7 key priority areas in order to focus the limited resources of the division.

The project brief specified the use of a Systems Thinking approach, but it cautioned that this had to be conducted indirectly and in an implicit manner. Given the tight time periods allotted for study workshops and given the lack of familiarity of the participants with Systems Thinking, this posed a challenging facilitation task.

The Approach

To begin, a series of workshops were designed in consultation with the division manager. The issue was sensitive and contentious and so a consensus decision seemed well out of reach. Accordingly, management was hoping to reach a quick and *acceptable* decision.

The workshop methodology employed a Group Model Building (GMB) process using Systems Thinking. This involved a three-step process

101

starting with individual, silent brainstorming using the KJ technique[1] to identify the priority areas and cluster them into affinity groups. Next, the priority areas/clusters were converted into variables and used by the participants to construct causal loop diagrams representing systems of priorities (in contrast to a list of priorities). Finally, through a group process, leverage points or key priorities were identified and translated into new work designs.

When conducting a Group Model Building session, one should be aware that cognitive limitations, differences in perceptions, and ineffective communication patterns can block productive discussion and play a key role in the success or failure of interventions. Thus, the process requires expert facilitation skills to engender appropriate attitudes and skills for effective group dynamics to reach desired outcomes.

Identification of Issues

In the first instance, it was necessary to establish an open and safe ground for discussion and group dialogue. This required a shared understanding of what the real and perceived issues were. To elicit this, the following question was proposed and agreed upon by the group for brainstorming.

Workshop Question 1: *What is preventing us from making faster progress?*

Using the KJ methodology, a total of 50 'raw' statements were generated, or about five per participant. Then, using the silent mode of KJ, the participants clustered these statements into 19 headings. Figure 13 shows two examples of the affinity groupings of issues.

This exercise served as preparation for the next step, namely, identification of priority areas. The question of priority identification is often contentious in organizations as it implies trade-off decisions must be made, resulting in winners and losers. Thus the outcomes could be

---

[1]For more details on KJ or Affinity Method, see Maani and Cavana (2007) *Systems Thinking System Dynamics — Managing Change and Complexity*, Pearson Education, Prentice Hall, 2nd edition.

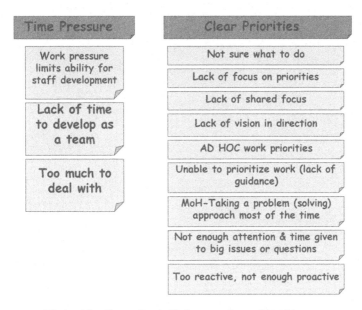

Figure 13.   Example of affinity groupings of 'raw' issues.

challenged openly or, worse, could be easily overlooked in silent resentments, resulting in loss of commitments to organizational decisions and actions.

In Systems Thinking, individual priorities are viewed as being part of a holistic and interdependent system of relationships. Hence, in contrast to the common notion that priority decisions have to be a 'zero-sum' game, they are viewed as part of a connected system where win-win solutions are plausible.

Identifying Key Priorities

The next step of the exercise was identifying key work priorities. The workshop question to solicit this was:

Workshop Question 2: *What are the priorities in health policy in terms of where the division should be placing its greatest efforts?*

Again the KJ methodology was used to identify 'raw' statements by each participant and then cluster them into 'key' priority areas. It is

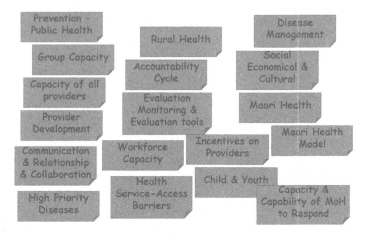

Figure 14.   High level priority areas.

important to note that the silent mode of KJ clustering is very beneficial in this process. Not only does it avoid awkward verbal disagreements and contradictions, it also converges opinions quickly, yielding visible group agreement and consensus. Furthermore, the participants view the process as fun, adding further motivation for group think and team building.

As the group represented diverse organizational hierarchies and professional backgrounds, it was important that no work areas were dismissed or reduced early on and prematurely. The KJ process ensured that all contributions were included, maximizing the 'airtime' for all participants. This exercise produced 42 'raw' priority statements, which were clustered into 18 priority areas, as shown in Figure 14.

Priority Selection

As the management objective was to select six to seven priority areas, it was necessary to reduce this list to six to seven areas. To do this, a set of criteria for priority selection had to be formulated. This was done through a multi-pick method whereby participants proposed a list of criteria. These criteria were then scrutinized and articulated further by the group. This process resulted in seven criteria as shown in Table 1.

Table 1. Criteria for priority selection.

1. Realistic — Can we marshal the resources? Is it reasonable and compatible with the Government's direction/political environment?
2. Impact — direct impact on Maori health
3. Quick visible results — within a few weeks or months (maximum six months)
4. Alignment — with the division's mission and other stakeholders
5. Fundamental cause — "Cause not symptom focus"
6. Existing initiatives — aligns with and capitalizes on existing initiatives
7. Planning horizon — short, medium or long

To apply these criteria objectively, a ranking matrix was used to rate the priorities. For simplicity, it was decided that these criteria were of equal weight (i.e., of equal importance). An ordinal ranking system of 1–5 was chosen where 1 indicated a low priority and 5 represented a high priority. The group then proceeded to rank each of the priority areas against the seven criteria. The outcome of this process is summarized in the priority matrix in Table 2.

According to the priority matrix, a clear set of rank-ordered priories emerged. As all of the participants had agreed to every step of the process to this point, it was expected that top priority areas would be readily selected from the priority matrix. Contrary to this expectation, the majority of the participants expressed strong objections to the top priority areas. This was both surprising and enlightening! Of course, no employee was prepared to let go of his or her area of work. While it was possible for the manager to intervene and use her authority to 'force' or coerce the opposing voices into acceptance, it was apparent that any such action would be counterproductive and damaging to the division's integrity and unity.

In general, it is important to remember that in groups where there are diverse tasks and multiple purposes, this resistance exists whether it is voiced or not. Here, the participants' outright rejection of the exercise's outcomes led the managers to resort to the Systems Thinking approach to break the impasse.

Table 2. Priority matrix.

Priority area	Realistic	Impact on Maori health	Quick visible results	Alignment	Fundamental cause	Capitalise on other initiatives	Planning time	Score
Accountability cycle	5	4	5	5	2	5	s	26
Developing Maori models	4	3	3	5	5	4	s	24
Evaluate monitoring & evaluation tools	4	4	3	5	2	4	s	22
Rural health	3	4	2	3	3	4	l	19
Maori provider development	5	4	2	5	3	5	s,m,l	24
Maori workforce capacity	4	4	2	5	3	5	s,m,l	23
Communication relationship & collaboration	5	3	5	5	2	5		25
Increase Maori health putea	3	3	1	5	4	4		20
Disease mngt	2	5	2	5	3	3		20
High priority diseases	2	5	2	5	4	3		21
Incentive on providers	3	2	2	2	3	3		15
Capacity & capability of MoH to respond	3	2	3	4	2	3		17
Social, cultural & economic	3	4	1	5	5	5		23
Child & youth	4	5	4	5	5	4		27
Access barriers	2	5	2	5	4	3		21
Whanau capacity	3	3	2	5	5	3		21
Treaty of Waitangi	3	4	3	5	5	3		23
Capacity of all providers	3	3	2	3	3	3		17
Prevention, public health	4	4	3	4	5	4		24
								0

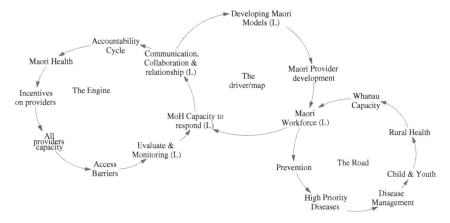

Figure 15. CLD showing the priorities as an interrelated system.

Priorities as System

To progress the project, and contrary to their initial mandate, management agreed not to pursue the reduction of work areas. Instead they agreed to use the Systems Thinking approach to resolve this conflict. As discussed earlier, the core philosophy of Systems Thinking is the primacy of relationships rather than focusing on the individual parts in isolation.

At the outset, management viewed staff work areas as independent units competing for resources. The critical mental shift occurred when the manager and the staff were asked to imagine their work areas as indispensable and connected parts of the organizational system. With this new mindset, the group, using their rudimentary knowledge of systems modeling, converted the priority areas into a CLD or systems of priorities. This is shown in Figure 15.

The CLD of priorities has three reinforcing loops, labeled as the Engine, the Road, and the Driver/Map. The overall CLD represents the central influence of the culture and broader socio-economic environment. This 'poetic' metaphor provided a powerful hook and narrative that had a natural and cultural affinity with the group and was one that they could readily identify with.

In this model, while all parts of the system may not be *equally* important, they all contribute to the functioning and efficacy of the whole. As discussed in Part 1, in Systems Thinking the relative importance of the parts is established through leverage points in the system. In this case, the participants collectively identified the leverage points as the work areas that had a key role and influence on the outcome of the organization. These are shown on the CLD by 'L' for leverage points.

To implement the new approach, the division formed teams of the staff with a clear focus on the leverage areas. This implied two important change management strategies. First, teamwork replaced the conventional individualized work design. Second, new work teams started focusing attention on leverage points as those areas could fundamentally change the underlying dynamics and long-term performance of the organization, realizing that a small shift in leverage points will have multiple chain effects in the system.

Conclusion

This case study illustrated the application of Group Model Building using Systems Thinking. The model building process catalyzed team learning and consensus decisions. The contentious issue of reducing work or priority areas, resulting from the conventional priority matrix, was overcome by a mental shift from priorities in isolation to priorities as an interrelated system. This was helped by using visual systems maps, which facilitated shared understanding of the issues and created a commitment to final decisions and action. Further, Systems Thinking led to team spirit, collective learning and creation of shared vision, collaboration, and cohesion within the division.

The methodology demonstrated here shows the power of Systems Thinking when used with novice users. The approach can be applied to other change management initiatives and complex decisions. The immediate and noticeable outcomes are shared vision and greater commitment to organizational and group decisions.

Case 4

Causes of Oversupply of Commercial Property — The Case of Singapore[1]

The Singapore commercial office market had an average vacancy rate of 6.2% at the end of 2012. This oversupply in the commercial real estate market was produced by a combination of a cyclic real estate market and strong supply side reactions to the various signals in the market. These supply side reactions were caused, in part, by political systems' interference in the real estate development process. While experienced real estate professionals have expertise in individual aspects of the development process, the inability to understand the interplay of these components within a complex system can often result in inadequate strategies based on the use of heuristic or judgment rules to simplify the decision-making process. This fragmentation of knowledge of building professionals, the building process, and the built environment is one of the fundamental problems of the Singapore building industry.

Real estate development is a complex process. Yet the industry, by and large, is still using traditional sub-optimal management tools to deal with the imbedded uncertainly and complexity. There are also entrenched individual and organizational "cognitive biases" that influence managers' judgment in investment decisions.

---

[1]Adapted from Patrina Chia Hui Pin's Systems Thinking Course final project, Aalto Executive MBA, 2013, Singapore.

Oversupply Dynamics

Several factors contribute to the oversupply of commercial buildings. Key factors are access to credit (financing), regulatory restrictions, the general economy, and barriers to entry. Several interconnected feedback loops capture these reciprocal relationships in Figure 16.

Easy access to credit results in an increase in the supply of office space, but when there is an oversupply the result is a credit crunch. This circular logic also applies to easing of regulatory restrictions, which is often done to stimulate building projects, but once overbuilding becomes a concern, regulatory restrictions become more severe. This same feedback logic exists between the general economy and the real estate economy, each affecting one another (e.g., overbuilding, savings and loan crisis). Barriers to entry are usually minimal during a boom, which leads to oversupply, which in turn feeds back to create stronger barriers to entry.

Patterns of Behavior (BoT)

After four quarters of positive net absorption, demand in the hitherto resilient Singapore office market relented in Q4 2012. According to real estate services and investment firm CBRE's estimates (see Figure 17), the final quarter of 2012 registered a net absorption of −354,886 square feet of commercial office space.

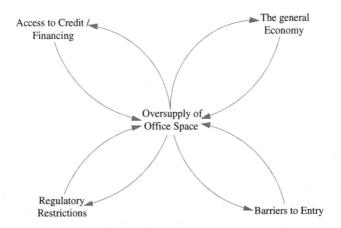

Figure 16.   Causes of office space oversupply.

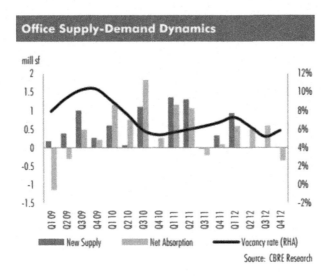

Figure 17.   Singapore supply and demand movements 2009–12.

Causal Loops

The dynamics of office space follow simple economics demand-supply laws. If the demand increases, the construction of office space will go up accordingly. As a result, the increase in the construction of office space increases the supply of office space and, in turn, an increase in the supply of office space decreases the demand for office space. As subsequent demand rises, so will construction, and so on. The net result is that an increase in demand for office space sets in motion a circular chain of events resulting in a decrease in demand, back to an equilibrium level. Therefore, it creates a self-regulating, balancing process as shown in Figure 18.

The balancing loop B1 in Figure 19 represents the basic business model of commercial real estate development. The reinforcing loop (R) shows two drivers of the price-induced demand; the investors' demand for commercial property and the market demand for office space. The investors' demand tends to be more speculative and aims to maximize asset appreciation due to inflation and/or speculative demand, often through products offered by financial institutions. While the R loop shows the dynamics of speculative pressure and/or the effects of financing on the number of constructions, B1 shows that as the property price goes up

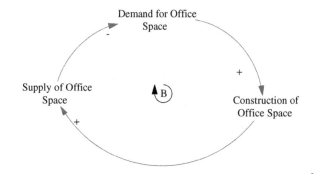

Figure 18. Basic demand-supply dynamics in real estate.

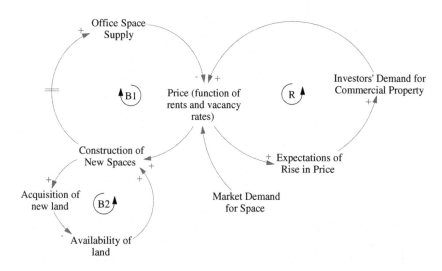

Figure 19. Commercial property development drivers.

construction of new buildings increases, whether or not the rise in price is caused by demand for space or investor's demand for buildings. New property developments will set off acquisition of land which in turn reduces the stock of available land. As shown in balancing loop (B2), this creates a constraint on further property development.

Effect of Delay

Delays are inherent in the real estate development process and are the main cause of structural boom-and-bust cycles in the industry. Hence, the real estate markets are subject to significant distortions due to time delays. The most critical part of this is the delay between a project start date and its completion and/or lease up. The market demand for office space can change drastically from the time that the decision is made to initiate a project to the time when that project is completed.

This structural delay cannot be avoided. While it may be reduced somewhat it will most likely become longer due to increasing processing times for regulatory approval. Pre-leasing of space prior to construction, in lieu of speculative building, can mitigate the delay-induced market risk to a great extent. However, tenants who are both willing and able to make location decisions three to seven years in advance may be rare. This delay in the feedback process is one of the prime structural reasons for the cyclicality of the real estate industry.

In addition to construction-related delays, there are also information and response delays to market signals, particularly in the commercial office market. Hence, in commercial real estate, the developer must compensate by obtaining a better understanding of market dynamics.

Mental Models

Interviews were conducted with professionals in commercial leasing, projects and business development, and financial analysis. The objective was to determine how they used both experience and analytic tools to arrive at the decision of whether or not to build. The format was informal and unstructured in order to draw out their candid responses and mental models.

The interviews were intended to obtain insights into the professionals':

- level of systemic understanding of the industry,
- internal versus external orientation,
- relative use of intuition versus analytical methods in decision making,
- length of decision time horizons: short versus long term, and
- identification of conceptual blocks that influence the formation of developers' mental models.

1) Knowledge Bias
The participants showed bias towards overemphasis of their understanding of the local market in their decision making. The more-in depth

knowledge of the local economic variables they had, the more confident they were in their judgment.

This knowledge of the local market, while necessary, only provides a shallow understanding of the detail complexity of the marketplace. The over-confidence gained by possessing this detailed knowledge hid the developer's lack of understanding of the dynamic complexity.

2) Detailed versus Dynamic Complexity

While a detailed understanding of the complexity of the market provides a competitive advantage, it does not translate into an understanding of the dynamic complexity of the real estate development system. Development decisions are commonly based on market conditions at the time of the analysis, hence subsequent changes in the demand and the supply side of the market are overlooked.

3) Understanding of Systemic Structures

Generally, developers were unable to articulate an explicit understanding of the cyclical behavior of the real estate market being caused by internal structure of the system, specifically the supply side response to external demand.

It appears that the external orientation most developers possess inhibits understanding the systemic nature of the industry — a mental block that appears to be difficult for the developers and investors to overcome.

4) Causes of Oversupply

Easily obtainable financing was identified as a primary cause of an over-built market which encouraged speculative building for investment rather than building to fulfill user demand. Also, developers like to build — their expertise, pride, and sense of accomplishment are found in the building process. According to one financial analyst:

Easy lending practices have also contributed to the oversupply. Lenders, financial institutions, and developers all had overconfidence in 2005/06 growth in office employment. Of course developer's ego had a part to play as well.

This 'emotional' thinking also led the developers to neglect managing their developments as a capital asset, notwithstanding the fact that capital expenditure could become the demise of a leveraged project.

As decision makers, real estate developers need to synthesize information and knowledge about numerous variables, such as local supply and demand, macro supply and demand, financing, regulation, construction, and leasing. This is extremely complex when the variables are static, even more so in reality, when these variables are continuously changing. In practice, however, the common strategy is to use intuitive judgment or heuristics.

In summary, the survey of the developers revealed the following mental models:

- Developers have a poor understanding of the internal dynamics of the commercial real estate industry.
- Developers rely heavily on intuition. Often this intuition resulted in the conceptual block of stereotyping or looking for information that supported predetermined mental models.
- Real estate is a capital asset that has a long life span, yet developers have difficulty making decisions today based on a future so far away.

This highlights the need to rethink the critical role of the developers in the real estate industry. Systems Thinking allows developers to better intuit the complexity of the real estate development. Understanding the systemic structure underlying the real estate development market helps industry decision makers to unravel the dynamic nature of the market and how to avoid common decision pitfalls.

Tacit knowledge and mental models

One of Systems Thinking's values lies in converting *tacit* knowledge into explicit and shared knowledge and understanding. However, this value is realized when the newly gained understandings are internalized into the mental models of managers. This is an area of leverage in influencing deep organizational change, as it is the mental models that underlie the behavior and actions of decision makers.

In the real estate industry, there are several mental blocks that can be associated with the developer's narrow view of their business in relation to the market. One of these blocks is the endemic difficulties in isolating problems. Often, developers can become so absorbed in solving the problem of how to get the project built that they do not question if it should be built in the first place. Developers tend to be action-oriented, and while this has led to their success, it can also lead to their misreading of market signals. While an important attribute of success at project level, the "can-do" attitude can be a downfall from a long range strategic perspective. The developer has a "project" orientation. This causes a lack of long-term strategy that takes into account the cyclic nature of real estate, macro and micro economic factors influencing the demand, and the cumulative effects of building. The project drive focuses on the financials of an individual deal, rather than the underlying economies of the capital asset. This is further complicated by the fact that, in the real estate industry, the delay between the decision to develop and the completion, sale, or lease-up of a project is usually a minimum of three years, making it difficult to evaluate the impact of decisions objectively at the outset.

Decision makers tend to see what they want to see. This is why they ignore, dismiss, or fail to recognize any information that is inconsistent with established beliefs. Decision makers also often fail to see how the cumulative effects of individual actions contribute to the final outcome. Further, gradual processes often go unnoticed until it is too late. The signals of an impending bust may appear obvious later, but they are ignored at that time. Finally, line managers can see the signals that the market is changing, but are not motivated to present the findings to higher authority, particularly if it conflicts with the upper management's current perception.

Summary

This study shed light on the dynamics of decision making in the commercial real estate market. It revealed that the players in the Singapore real estate industry: (1) have a poor systemic understanding of the real estate development process, (2) have an external orientation as to the cause of the problems in the real estate development industry, (3) use intuition and judgment over analytical methods for decision making, (4) have a surprisingly short-term perspective for such a long-life asset, and (5) are influenced by individual and organizational learning disabilities which prevent them from improving the mental models of the real estate development as a system and their place in it. Systems Thinking can help overcome these cognitive biases and conceptual barriers to organizational learning.

Case 5

The Blind Spots
of Increased Factory Capacity[1]

Ziron[2] is a world leader in the design and manufacture of electronic equipment, supplying printed circuit boards (PCBs), and customized products to original equipment manufacturers (OEMs), original design manufacturers (ODMs), and contract equipment manufacturers (CEM). To support its sales and service around the world, Ziron has established a global network to provide direct support services to its customers. These services include training, application support, installation, and maintenance that are available to customers around the clock, all year long, and anywhere in the world. Moreover, to meet the latest technology trends, Ziron provides a world class R&D design laboratory with optimal output/ accuracy ratios.

Service quality is a key determinant for customers in selecting a vendor. This is especially important for manufacturing companies in which revenue depends on the performance and reliability of manufacturing equipment. Therefore, providing high quality service at lower costs is the critical issue for Ziron. These services include a pre-install check and installation support, technical training, round-the-clock on-site support

---

[1]Adapted from Nina Chou's final project for the System Thinking for Managers Course, Helsinki School of Economics Executive MBA, 2006, Taipei.
[2]Fictitious name for a global company.

119

for three years, spare parts consignment, and application support to meet customers' special requests (customized solutions).

These are costly activities, especially the skilled labor and spare parts components. Furthermore, in order for the company to adopt new technology trends to deliver higher output with frequent changeovers, Ziron must develop and deliver increasingly more complex products and associated software as well as new consultancy and support services.

The Challenge

With rapid technological changes and ever decreasing profit margins, how can manufacturers deliver more value to customers and remain competitive?

Key Variables

The starting point for Ziron to gain a systemic understanding of this challenge is to identify the relevant variables and their interconnectedness.

Technology trend: Due to continuous advances in electronics technology, component sizes are getting smaller and smaller, which makes the accuracy requirement and performance of equipment more demanding. Key variables of this trend are:

• Component size
• Accuracy requirement on equipment

Manufacturing process: Depending on the complexity of the product, the following variables play a part in the overall performance of the manufacturing process:

• Defect rate
• Machine down time
• Operator's learning curve

Service quality: Due to the nature of the production line, round-the-clock service needs to be provided in order to guarantee customer satisfaction. Variables here include:

• Consignment parts
• Customer service turn over

- Training for new customer service staff
- Equipment serviceability

The behavior over time (BOT) graphs in Figure 20 show key trends in the above variables.

Behavior Over Time (BOT) Graphs

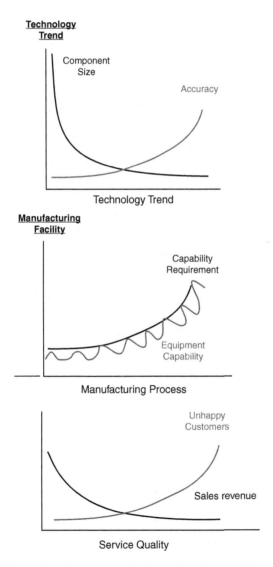

Figure 20.   Behavior over time graphs of key variables.

Causal Loop Diagrams (CLDs)

New technology trends create a constant gap between the latest high performance technology and Ziron's current equipment capability. The purchase of new equipment and upgrading of existing equipment reduces this gap, for a while, until the next wave of new technology occurs and creates a new gap. This dynamic is shown in the balancing loop (B1) in Figure 21.

Once new equipment is installed, factory capacity is increased. Because of the increased capacity, the company receives more orders, which raises the workload of the operators. This, in turn, constrains factory capacity, as shown in loop B2 in the CLD in Figure 22. The increasing workload of operators directly results in higher product defect rates and also increased downtime of equipment. These effects further hamper the factory capacity, as shown in loops B4 and B3 respectively. The increasing level of defects triggers the need for training to resolve product quality problems, which in time restores some production capacity (the R loop).

With growing sales of equipment, Ziron needs to provide more on-site support staff to customers. Even after new machines have been installed, customers still require certain criteria to be met before payment for the equipment is made. This could take more than three months, so it is in the interest of the company to meet these requirements in a speedy and satisfactory fashion.

Consequently, customer support (CS) workload and pressures increase concomitantly. Over time, this results in a higher turnover of CS staff, which hinders service quality and creates unhappy customers. This arrests

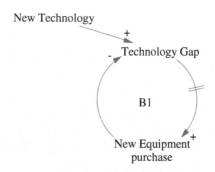

Figure 21. Technology trends loop.

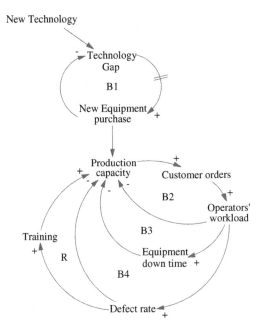

Figure 22.   On-site supporting loops.

sales, revenue, and the company's ability to upgrade and acquire new technology. These dynamics are shown in the CLD in Figure 23.

Customer satisfaction loop

In the electronic equipment industry, customer satisfaction is especially important for a successful business. With satisfied customers, new orders continue to rise and sales revenue increases. On-site and continual customer support is tantamount to service quality, which sustains customer satisfaction and further sales. In order to support and sustain satisfaction to new customers, more engineers need to be hired. This dynamic can be shown in the reinforcing loop in Figure 24.

Leverage Point

An examination of the CLDs presented in this case study make it clear that service quality is the key to growing sales revenue and creating a

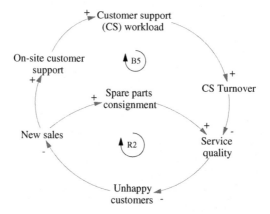

Figure 23. Customer satisfaction dynamics.

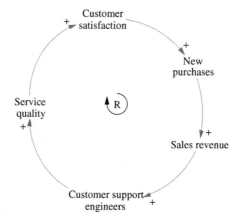

Figure 24. Service quality and customer satisfaction.

larger customer base. In order to enhance the service quality, adequately qualified customer support engineers are needed to provide technical advice and training, rather than only placing consignment parts on the customer's site.

Mental Model

Accepting service quality as the key leverage point for growth is counterintuitive to Ziron's culture and the mental model of its managers. Specifically, common beliefs within this mental model are reflected in the employees' verbatim comments below.

- *Increasing equipment capacity will necessarily increase productivity.* However, the fact is that if the workforce is not adequately trained for the new equipment, productivity will not increase commensurately.
- *More consignment parts or more customer support engineers at the customer's site will solve the on-site support quality issues and reduce unhappy customers.* Actually, this is not about the *quantity* of support staff; rather it is the quality. Without improving support workforce quality, customers will not be happy in the long term.

The above lessons are true for most companies, especially service-oriented ones where enhancing service quality is the key to increasing profits and continuous growth. This requires investments in recruiting more support staff and providing adequate training to the support workforce.

Case 6

Dynamics of Worldwide Fisheries Decline[1]

The decline in world fisheries is a global issue that has caused deep concerns for international organizations such as the Food and Agriculture Organization of the United Nations (FAO) and the World Resources Institute (WRI). The rapid increase in fish landings has caused the decline and depletion of major fish stocks, making overfishing an international problem. Before the 1950s, the problem was limited to a few regions including the North Atlantic, the North Pacific, and the Mediterranean. However, since the 1950s, the expansion of global fishing activities has resulted in the exploitation of fish stocks globally. As a result, many fishing areas have reached their maximum productivity and are in decline. Although policy makers and industry groups have paid some attention to this problem, a drastic change in fisheries policy and management is urgently needed.

According to the FAO, 60% of the world's important fish stocks need to be managed and rehabilitated. The fish harvest records from 1950 to 1994 indicate that 35% of the most important commercial fish stocks experienced decreasing yields and require actions to stop the exploitation of fisheries. In addition, another 25% of fish stocks are harvested at their biological limits. Overall, the world's fish stock has dropped from 14 million metric tons in 1985 to 8 million metric tons in 1998 (WRI 2009a, 2009b).

---

[1]Adapted from Vanessa L. Tosteson and Thanh Le Cong's final project for the Systems Thinking for Sustainability Course, 2009, The University of Queensland.

Worldwide, fish accounts for 20% of all animal protein in the human diet and fish products exceed the total production from poultry, beef, or pork. Research indicates that the global fish supply will decline in the next two decades due to the increasing demand for fish and the depletion of natural fish stocks. It is estimated that demand for fish exceeds current fish stocks by between 37%–50% (WRI 2009a and 2009b).

Furthermore, fisheries and related activities provide income to 30 million people globally and 95% of this employment is based in developing countries (UNEP 2009). The decline of fisheries impacts employment in these countries, especially small-scale fishers who catch fish for the domestic market and their subsistence. In the past two decades about ten million fishers have lost their business due to the growth of commercial vessels (WRI 2009a). The following quote sums up the problem:

> *Right now, no one is winning. The real income levels of fishers are depressed, much of the industry is unprofitable, fish stocks are depleted, and other sectors of the economy foot the bill for an ailing fishing industry* (World Bank 2008; cited by EWG 2009).

Purpose of the Study

This study aims to: 1) identify the key variables related to the decline of global fisheries, 2) track the behavior of the key variables over time, 3) build causal loop diagrams to investigate the relationships between the variables, 4) determine the key leverage points for potential interventions in the system, and 5) recommend intervention strategies that could change the whole system.

Key Variables

Figure 25 identifies the key variables that explain the decline of global fisheries and each variable is briefly defined in the following paragraphs.

Landings is defined as *"the amount of fish brought back to the docks and marketed. Landings can describe the kept catch of one vessel, of an entire fishery, or of several fisheries combined."* (NRDC n.d). Landings is measured in million tons of fish caught per year.

Figure 25.   Key variables and their unit of measure.

Discards are the amount of fish caught and returned to the sea. Usually these are fish that are below the minimum landing size, species that are protected, or restrictions due to quota limits. Discards can be up to one-third of the annual total catch; hence the management of fisheries is often based on incorrect information (Pauly *et al.* 2002).

Fish stock is generally defined as: *"characteristics of semi-discrete groups of fish with some definable attributes which are of interest to fishery managers"* (Begg *et al.* 1999 p. 3). For this project the characteristic of interest is "exploitation" of fish stock — over-exploited, fully exploited or under-exploited.

Subsidies are *"government actions or inactions outside of normal practices that modify — by increasing or decreasing — the potential profits by the fisheries industry in the short-, medium- or long-term"* (Westlund, 2004 Chapter 4). This variable is important because it has been linked to increasing overcapacity and overfishing. Fuel subsidies are especially important for trawling fisheries.

Consumption measures the quantity of fish consumed in a period of time. Consumption is important because fish is a major source of food worldwide, providing animal protein to almost one sixth of the global population (BBC 2002).

Fishery-related jobs describes the employment in the fisheries sector worldwide. The focus in this study is on the jobs lost due to declining fisheries, which is an important socio-economic indicator of the impacts of overfishing.

Trophic level (TL) identifies the level of the fish species in the marine food chain. TL is smallest for species in the bottom of the marine food chain such as algae and increases to higher levels for herbivorous fish and is the highest for carnivorous fish species. TL is an important variable as it is a clear indicator of fisheries sustainability (Pauly *et al.* 2002).

Size of fish in landings describes the weight or length of fish caught in any fishery. It is an important indicator because fisheries tend to diminish the size of fish, which is a sign of overfishing.

Behavior Over Time (BoT) for Key Variables

Landings

The global marine production of fish has steadily increased since 1950, reaching a peak around the late 1980s (Figure 26; the corrected data from 1988 to 1998 is due to China's over-reporting (Helfman 2007, p. 256)). The recent decline in fish production is evidence of worldwide overfishing in the oceans.

Overfishing has led to the collapse of the commercial harvest of several important fish stocks in the Northwest Atlantic, originally red hake and recently Atlantic cod and haddock as per Figure 27 (FAO 1997 cited by WRI 2009a).

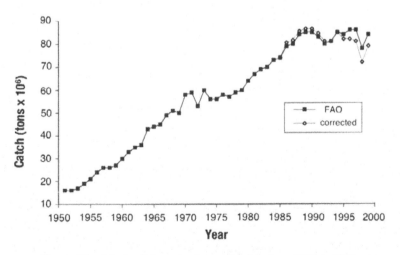

Figure 26.   Marine fish production worldwide from 1950 to 2000.

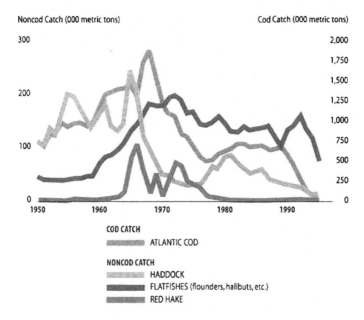

Figure 27. Northwest Atlantic fish stocks that have collapsed due to overfishing.

Discards (Tonnes/Yr)

Discards are usually not reported as part of the landings of a fishery, nevertheless they are important as they contribute to the total catch measure. The trend for total discards follows a similar pattern as total landings shown in Figure 26. Discards have increased from a few million tons per year in 1950 to more than 20 million tons per year in 1988 and relatively stable since then (Pauly *et al.* 2002).

Fish Stock (Biomass)

According to the FAO, 80% of commercial fish stocks are overexploited and threatened. Specifically, 19% are overexploited, 52% are fully exploited, 8% are significantly depleted, and 1% is recovering (UNEP 2009). Figure 28 shows the trends for fish stock or biomass as the percentage of overexploited, depleted or recovering fish stocks has increased from the mid-1970s to 2005, while the percentage of underexploited and

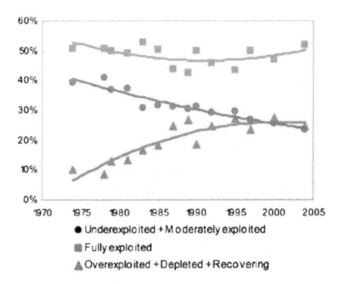

Figure 28. Graph showing percentage of exploitation of fish stocks in world fisheries (World Bank n.d.).

moderately exploited has decreased, and the fully exploited stocks have remained more or less constant. Furthermore, the FAO (2008) reported that *"The stocks of the top ten species, which together account for about 30 percent of world marine capture fisheries production in terms of quantity, are fully exploited or overexploited"* (UNEP, 2009 p. 7).

Subsidies

Fishing subsidies have been described as a global problem. They are estimated to be in excess of US$30 billion per year. In the USA alone, fisheries subsidies amounted to approximately US$6.5 billion between 1996 and 2004 and fuel subsidies made up 44% of the total fishing subsidies (EWG 2009).

Consumption

Global fish consumption has almost doubled in nearly 50 years, and there would have to be a doubling of catches to meet the demand for fish. Further, in developing countries, fish is an increasing source of protein;

hence demand is surpassing supply (BBC 2002). The global trend of per capita consumption of fish increased from 9.9 kg per person in the 1960s to 16.4 kg in 2005 (GreenFacts 2009).

Fishery-related jobs

For decades, fisheries jobs have been in steady decline. In 1992 alone, Canada lost 40,000 jobs due to the collapse of the cod fishery (Greenpeace n.d.). Likewise, Norway's fisheries employment has been steadily decreasing since 1996 as shown in Figure 29.

Trophic level (TL) in fisheries landings

The mean trophic level of fisheries landings for both the North Atlantic and global coasts has decreased dramatically from 1970 to 2000 (Pauly & Watson 2005), as shown in Figure 30. As mentioned earlier, the average TL of fisheries landings is useful as an indicator of sustainability of fisheries in marine ecosystems. Fishers tend to take large fish at the top of the

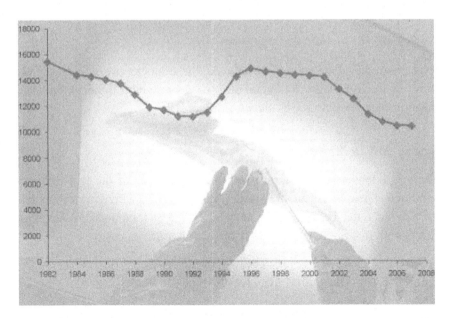

Figure 29.   Employment figures in the fisheries industry of Norway (Nofima Marine 2008).

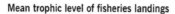

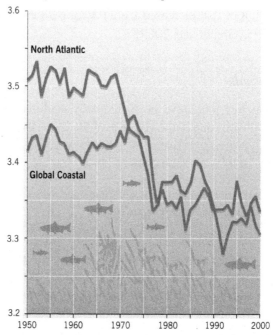

Figure 30. Mean trophic level in fisheries landings from 1950 to 2000. (*Source*: Pauly and Watson 2005 cited by Greenfacts 2009).

food chain first (e.g., sharks, tuna). As these stocks are depleted, fish lower on the food chain are fished next (e.g., mackerel, flounder), thus the mean trophic level drops, as shown in Figure 30.

Size of fish in landings

There is a tendency in fisheries to diminish the size of the fish that are exploited. There has been an 88% decrease in landed weight of top predator fish since the 1950s. Figure 31 shows three historical photographs of fish caught in competitive sports fishing in Florida.

Causal Loop Diagrams and Key Loops

For this study three sub-systems were identified as part of the fisheries decline worldwide: "socio-economic", "governmental policies", and

Figure 31. Historical photographs of trophy fish caught in Key West, Florida. (a) 1957, (b) Early 1980s, and (c) 2007. (*Source*: Science Daily 2009).

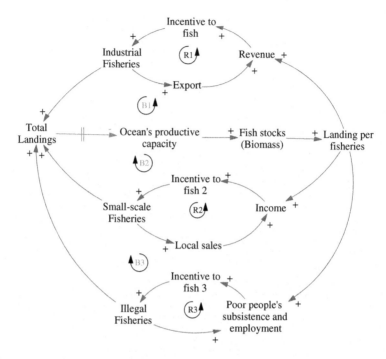

Figure 32. "The Tragedy of the Commons" in global fisheries.

"environmental" loops, comprising 13 reinforcing and 4 balancing loops. Two key archetypes or generic system models are also present here, namely a "tragedy of the commons" and "limits to success".

The "socio-economic" loop is explained by the "Tragedy of the Commons" (Hardin 1968) in Figure 32, when a common resource such as fish is over-exploited because of open and unregulated access. The fishing behaviors of industrial, small-scale, and illegal fishers collectively contribute to the total landings in worldwide fisheries, although each group's behavior is reinforced by different motives and factors. For example, industrial fishers are generally driven by export markets (loop R1), while the fishing patterns for small-scale fishers are affected in part by local markets, local consumption and overall benefits to the community (loop R2). Illegal fishers are motivated by subsistence income and fisheries-related employment to reduce poverty (loop R3). An important connection also exists between industrial and small-scale fisheries. An increasing number of small-scale fishing vessels are being replaced by industrial ones, thus reducing the number of small-scale fishers. This further reinforces the incentives for industrial fisheries to fish more to realize the return on their investment.

In summary, the "tragedy of the commons" explains how excessive landings observed globally from 1950 to the late 1980s (per Figure 26) have decreased the ocean's productive capacity over time and, consequently, today over 80% of fish stocks are overexploited. This, in turn, has decreased landings and hence economic gain in the industry, which has forced governments worldwide to continue to subsidize the fishing industry.

Another important dynamic connected to the tragedy of the commons is the "limits to growth" dynamic shown in Figure 33. As can be seen at the top of Figure 33, population and economic growth lead to higher demand and consumption, which are the key drivers behind total fishing activity resulting in more landings and hence revenue (the "growth " loop R4). Further, increases in standards of living have boosted fish consumption worldwide. Here, the *limit* to the "growth" is the reproductive capacity of the ocean (loop B4). However, the long lag time between increased landings and decreased ocean's productive capacity obscures this pattern, making it difficult to institute timely interventions to arrest this trend.

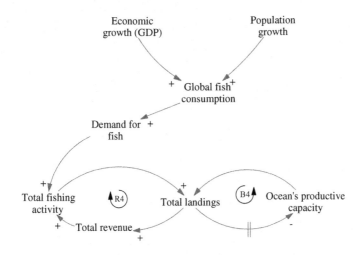

Figure 33. Global fisheries "Limits to Growth."

Government policies loop

In addition to the factors discussed above, government policies, especially in the form of subsidies, have contributed to the decline of fisheries. Declining fish stocks and subdued economic gains for the industry have encouraged governments to increase subsidies for the fishers, lowering operational costs and boosting modernization of the industry, which in turn has led to greater activity and landings (van den Bergh *et al*. 2006). In addition, overestimation of fish stocks has intensified total effort and landings, exacerbating the overexploitation of world fish stocks. These effects are shown via the reinforcing vicious cycle loop R5 in Figure 34.

In summary, past decisions of fisheries management have contributed to the global decline of fish stocks observed today. Some of the drivers behind the mismanagement of fisheries include a short-term view, lack of institutional political will, neglect of exploiters, and ignoring the limits of marine ecosystems, which results in setting wrong targets.

Environment loop

Increased landings significantly alter marine food webs and fish habitats by removing important predators from the ecosystem. This forces fishers to catch species that are located in lower trophic levels, also known as "bottom trawling". This 'simplifies' the food webs in marine systems, reducing the resilience of ecosystems to adapt to changes in environmental conditions

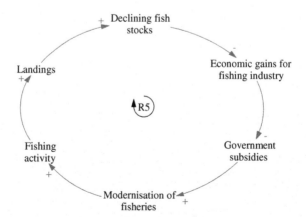

Figure 34.   Government policies loop.

such as climate change (Berkes *et al.* 2006). This reduces the survival of marine species and diminishes biodiversity, which decreases the ocean's productive capacity and shrinks total landings. The end result is a balancing cycle that self-regulates total fishing activity and landings over time. This is shown by loop B5 in Figure 35. The damage to marine ecosystems and loss of biodiversity is further exacerbated by exploiters' actions.

Mental models

This study highlights the main cause for the decline in fisheries to be the reinforcing loop of government policies. The "mental models" or "beliefs, values, and assumptions" held by governments and the fishing industry are by and large based on the convenient conviction that the ocean is limitless and it will forever supply our demands (Pauly *et al.* 2002). There is also widespread denial of the role and failure of management and institutions. The following quotes reflect some mental models of the industry and governments:

"Stocks are not declining, they are changing location" (Bigot 2002 cited by Pauly, Watson and Alder 2005, p. 6).

"We have this belief that we can knock down fish populations to exceedingly low levels and they can bounce back rapidly" (SeaWeb 2005)

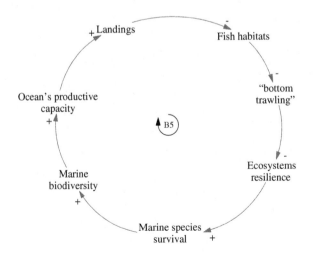

Figure 35. Landings and marine biodiversity.

Another mental model lies in the notion that decline of fish stocks is due to environmental variations and not to exploiters' actions (Pauly *et al.* 2002). Figure 36 illustrates contrasting mental models of governments who overestimate fish stocks to justify subsidies to the fishing industry, with scientists who report diminishing trends.

Leverage points

Leverage points are places or variables in a system that can change or break the vicious cycles. Meadows (1999) suggests that the most profound changes in a system are achieved by altering its goals and mindset, or paradigms of the decision makers. Numerous fisheries studies confirm the mindset and the critical role of governments in relation to fisheries. For example, *"the only way to reverse trends toward over-harvesting... is through large-scale government intervention ... to reduce aggregate fishing effort, and/or through the establishment of large marine protected areas"* (Murray *et al.* 2007, p. 82). Reducing or eliminating subsidies and the paradigm behind it could arrest the decline of the fisheries system and reverse the vicious cycles shown above.

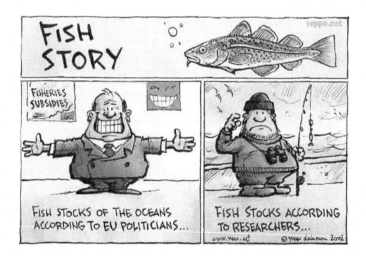

Figure 36. Cartoon illustrating researchers' and governments' lack of effective communication. (*Source*: Seppo n.d.).

Intervention strategies

This study shows the effect of government subsidies on the fishery industry, which have led to increased volumes of catch and landings that are biologically unsustainable. To arrest this trend and increase fish stocks (biomass) to sustainable levels, appropriate incentives must be put in place to minimize the over-capacity of the fishing industry.

Other measures include drastic fleet reductions of breaching fishers through taxation and facilitating the re-entry of small-scale fishers who have been removed from the industry (Pauly *et al.* 2002). These actions can avoid the negative social and economic impacts of removing subsidies and fishing fleets.

Another important intervention is the creation of marine protected areas (MPAs) with the inclusion of 'no-take' zones to rebuild fish stocks. Studies (Roberts *et al.* 2001; Pauly *et al.* 2002; Roberts 2003) have found that creating marine reserves can increase fish stocks between 46% and 90% within a short period of time. In this regard, increasing the number of MPAs worldwide and establishing a Global Network of MPAs that should cover at least 40% of the ocean as opposed to the current 1% (NRC 2001 cited by Roberts 2003) is paramount.

Other strategies include integrated policy and management approaches that consider the natural limits of ecosystems (e.g., effects of fishing on food webs), community-based management, and traditional knowledge of local fishers (Berkes, Colding & Folke 2000).

Further, as shown above, the chief failure of fisheries management has been to ignore the negative impact of the exploiters. Strategies to reduce the impact that fishers have on marine ecosystems include educational programs that enhance environmental awareness and proper consideration of actions by exploiters (Hilborn *et al.* 1995).

Summary and Conclusions

This case study examined the worldwide fisheries decline by investigating the interrelationships among social, economic, governmental, and environmental issues. To achieve this, identifying key variables and their trends over time was essential to find the causal relationships amongst them.

In summary, our analysis of global fisheries decline led to several causal loop diagrams that included "tragedy of the commons" and "limits to growth" archetypes. Collectively, these loops revealed several vicious cycles and balancing loops imbedded in a system that connected socio-economic, governmental, and environmental variables. Thus we were able to visualize the big picture behind the fisheries decline.

In contrast to the Systems Thinking method, the conventional group decision-making process depends on a single angle of the problem resulting in sub-optimum and symptomatic solutions. Additionally, when considering the whole system, changes in leverage variables result in a positive shift of the *entire* structure.

Our study revealed that fish has been considered a commodity and not a potentially diminishing source of food, especially in developing countries, as well as a significant contributor to the health of ecosystems. Treating fish stocks as products undermines their importance for both humanity and natural systems. For the fishing industry to regain sustainability this mentality needs to transform. The strategies proposed in this study include:

(1) Implementation of appropriate government policies that change the goal of subsidies to the fisheries sector from over-capacity or increased effort to supporting fishers and changes towards sustainable practices;

(2) Creation of marine protected areas (MPAs) and effective no-take zones including a Global Network of MPAs to not only enhance biodiversity but to increase the fish stocks as well;

(3) Considering the impact of exploiters and instituting environmental awareness programs to modify the behavior of fishers towards sustainable outcomes; and finally,

(4) Integrating ecosystem- and community-based management including traditional ecological knowledge to change the power structure of the system from governmental control to communities and fishers; together they can help transform the system to become one that is sustainable and has positive impacts for both human populations and marine ecosystems.

The Systems Thinking approach provided profound understanding and deep insights by investigating the underlying relationships within the fisheries system. Further, the causal loop diagrams were an extremely powerful tool to unravel the key drivers and the strategies that help change the system.

References

BBC. (2002, 31 October). Global fish crisis 'to worsen'. *BBC News.* Retrieved from http://news.bbc.co.uk/1/hi/sci/tech/2381559.stm

Begg, G. A., Friedland, K. D., & Pearce, J. B. (1999). Stock identification and its role in stock assessment and fisheries management: An overview. *Fisheries Research, 43*(1–3), 1–8.

Berkes, F., Colding, J. & Folke, C. (2000). Rediscovery of traditional ecological knowledge as adaptive management. *Ecological Applications, 10*(5), 1251–1262.

Berkes, F., Hughes, T. P., Steneck, R. S., Wilson, J. A., Bellwood, D. R., Crona, B., . . .Worm, B. (2006). Globalization, roving bandits, and marine resources. *Science, 311*(5767), 1557–1558.

EWG (Environmental Working Group). (2009). *On the hook: Commercial fishing reaps billions.* Retrieved from http://www.ewg.org/research/hook-commercial-fishing-reaps-billions

Greenfacts. (2009). *Trends in mean trophic levels of fisheries landings (1950–2000).* Retrieved from http://www.greenfacts.org/en/global-biodiversity-outlook/toolboxes/figure-2-10.htm

Hardin, G. (1968). The tragedy of the commons. *Science, 162*(3859), 1243–1248.

Helfman, G. S. (2007). *Fish conservation: A guide to understanding and restoring global aquatic biodiversity and fishery resources.* Washington, DC: Island Press.

Hilborn, R., Walters, C. J., & Ludwig, D. (1995). Sustainable exploitation of renewable resources. *Annual Review of Ecology and Systematics, 26,* 45–67.

Meadows, D. (1999). *Leverage points: Places to intervene in a system.* Hartland, VT: The Sustainability Institute.

Murray, G., Neis, B., & Schneider, D. C. (2007). Lessons from a multi-scale historical reconstruction of Newfoundland and Labrador fisheries. *Coastal Management, 36*(1), 81–108.

Nofima Marine. (2008). *Employment numbers unchanged.* Retrieved from http://en.fiskforsk.norut.no/layout/set/print/content/view/full/14682

NRDC (Natural Resources Defense Council). (n.d.). *Glossary of environmental terms.* Retrieved from http://www.nrdc.org/reference/glossary/l.asp

Pauly, D., Christensen, V., Guénette, S., Pitcher, T. J., Sumaila, U. R., Walters, C. J., Watson, R., & Zeller, D. (2002). Towards sustainability in world fisheries. *Nature, 418*, 689–695.

Pauly, D., & Watson, R. (2005). Background and interpretation of the 'marine trophic index' as a measure of biodiversity. *Philosophical Transactions of the Royal Society (Biological Sciences), 360*(1454), 415–423.

Pauly, D., Watson, R., & Alder, J. (2005). Global trends in world fisheries: Impacts on marine ecosystems and food security. *Philosophical Transactions of the Royal Society (Biological Sciences), 360*(1453), 5–12.

Roberts, C. M. (2003). Our shifting perspectives on the oceans. *Oryx, 37*(2), 166–177.

Roberts, C. M., Bohnsack, J. A., Gell, F., Hawkins, J. P., & Goodridge, R. (2001). Effects of marine reserves on adjacent fisheries, *Science, 294*(5548), 1920–1923.

Science Daily. (2009, 2 March). Historical photographs expose decline in Florida's reef fish, study finds. *Science News.* Retrieved from http://www.sciencedaily.com/releases/2009/02/090217141813.htm

SeaWeb. (2005, 9 March). New science sheds light on rebuilding fisheries. *Science News.* Retrieved from https://www.sciencedaily.com/releases/2005/02/050223155540.htm

Seppo. (n.d.). *Fish story.* Retrieved from http://www.seppo.net/cartoons/albums/cartoons/nature/fishes/wwf_liikakalastus_EU_2007_eng.jpg

UNEP (United Nations Environment Programme). (2009). *Fisheries subsidies and the WTO: Update and introductory briefing for new delegates.* Retrieved from http://www.unep.ch/etb/events/WTO%20FS%20workshop%201%20Apr%202009/UNEP-WWF%20fisheries%20subsidies%20briefing%20april1.pdf

van den Bergh, J. C. J. M., Hoekstra, J., Imeson, R., Nunes, P. A. L. D., & de Blaeij, A. T. (2006). *Bioeconomic modelling and evaluation of exploited marine ecosystems.* Springer: Dordrecht, The Netherlands.

Westlund, L. (2004). *Guide for identifying, assessing and reporting on subsidies in the fisheries sector* (FAO Fisheries Technical Paper 438). Rome, Italy: Food and Agriculture Organization of the United Nations.

World Bank. (n.d.). *The state of exploitation of fish stocks.* Retrieved from http://siteresources.worldbank.org/INTAGISOU/Images/Figure_6_1.gif

WRI (World Resources Institute). (2009a). *Diminishing returns: World fisheries under pressure.* Retrieved from http://www.nzdl.org/gsdl/collect/envl/archives/HASH0150/33a1eb95.dir/p196.jpg

WRI (World Resources Institute). (2009b). *Decline in fish stocks.* Retrieved from http://www.wri.org/publication/content/8385

Case 7

Sustainable Tourism and Poverty Alleviation — the Siem Reap Project

Siem Reap boasts Cambodia's Angkor Wat historical monument. Declared a UNESCO World Heritage site in 1992, Angkor Wat attracts over two million tourists annually. With about 60% of tourists to Cambodia visiting Siem Reap, the Government decided that tourism in the Siem Reap region is the key sector to lead Cambodia's economic growth. This was supported by a UNESCO pilot project in ecosystem tourism.

Siem Reap also features Tonle Sap Lake — the largest freshwater lake in Southeast Asia and a major fishing resource in the region. The lake covers an area of 250,000–300,000 hectares in the dry season and 1.0–1.6 million hectares in the wet season. Tonle Sap's water depth is 1–2 meters in the dry season and 8–11 meters in the wet season, creating the world-famous floating villages (see Figure 37). Approximately 62% of Tonle Sap's water is from the Mekong River and the rest originates from the Tonle Sap basin. The lake is a crucial flood regulator as it absorbs 20% of floodwaters from the Mekong River. Tonle Sap contains at least 200 species of fish, 42 species of reptiles, 225 species of birds, and 46 species of mammals.[1] It supports one of the world's most productive freshwater fisheries and provides nearly 70% of the protein intake of Cambodia's population.

Due to its rich biodiversity, UNESCO has declared the Tonle Sap (TS) basin as a Biosphere Reserve. The TS basin includes 81,800 km^2 or 45% of

---

[1] Asia Development Bank (ADB) Report, 2005.

147

Figure 37. Floating Village in Tonle Sap in the dry season.

total land area of Cambodia. The Minister of Tourism has mandated the need for a master plan to link Siem Reap with other parts of Cambodia, as well as Thailand and Vietnam, and integrate several projects for tourism development in the Siem Reap region and the Tonle Sap Biosphere Reserve.

The Siem Reap Project

At the invitation of the Cambodian Ministry of Tourism, a team of researchers from the University of Queensland (UQ)[2] engaged with government officials and staff in a two-year project involving a large group of local stakeholders as well as some NGOs. As part of this project, a group of Ministry staff and managers were sent to the University for training on Systems Thinking and related skill development courses. The training activity was part of the Learning Lab model that had been developed for the

---

[2]The University of Queensland (UQ) research team comprised Professors K. Maani and O. Bosch and Dr Nam Nguyen.

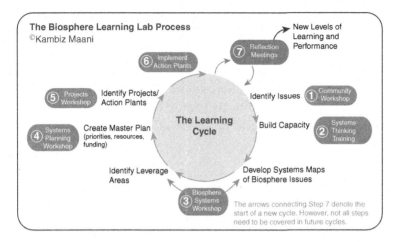

Figure 38. The Learning Lab Process.

UNESCO biosphere project in Hai Long Bay in Vietnam.[3] The Biosphere Learning Lab model is shown in Figure 38.

The Learning Lab Process

The application of the Learning Lab (LLab)[4] for sustainability follows a cyclical process for integrating cross-sectorial decision making, planning, and collaboration in dealing with complex multi-stakeholder integrated decision making and planning. The LLab comprises seven steps, explained below, whereby decision makers and stakeholders come together to develop a shared understanding of complex issues and create innovative and sustainable solutions. These steps can be customised for different projects and may take place in different sequences.

1. Community Workshop
Purpose: to identify key issues, problems, and challenges (e.g., social, economic, environmental, governance, leadership).

---

[3]Nguyen, N., Bosch, O. Maani, K., (2011) "Creating 'learning laboratories' for sustainable development in biospheres: A systems thinking approach", *Systems Research and Behavioral Science*, 28, 51–62.
[4]Maani K. and Cavana R. (2007) *Systems Thinking System Dynamics — Managing Change and Complexity*, Pearson Education, Prentice Hall, 2nd edition.

Participants: key decision makers and representatives from stakeholder groups including NGOs and the local community.

2. Systems Thinking Training

Purpose: to build Systems Thinking knowledge and skills for key decision makers in order to become directly involved in the next steps.

Participants: representative biosphere officials, policy makers, scientists, etc.

3. Systems Workshop

Purposes:

- to verify and validate the biosphere systems map/model
- to understand systemic issues and their interdependencies, and the role and responsibility of each stakeholder group
- to discuss and understand the implications for coordinated actions, strategy, and policy
- to identify key leverage areas for systemic interventions/change (based on the systems models)

Participants: key decision makers and representatives from stakeholder groups including the local community.

4. Planning Workshop

Purpose: to develop a Systemic Master Plan including priorities, funding, and provision of resources. The Systemic Master Plan will integrate with and supplement existing plans.

Participants: relevant decision makers including selected biosphere officials and representatives from government ministries, the private sector, NGOs, and donor organizations.

5. Projects/Funder Workshop

Purpose: to identify key projects based on leverage areas, and to design implementation plans. This step also includes a donor's workshop to seek financial assistance from potential local and international donors.

Participants: selected biosphere officials, technical officers, scientists, and representatives from affected stakeholders, NGOs, and donor organizations.

6. Implementation

Purpose: to implement projects, programs, and experiments. It is important to view this step as a "learning exercise" in which relevant NGOs and stakeholders participate in action steps stemming from their respective plans/strategies. As such, both success and failure become sources of learning and not a cause for blame or despair.

Participants: relevant NGOs, scientists, donor representatives, and stakeholders.

7. Reflection Meetings

Purpose: to monitor progress, identify drivers/causes of success and failure, and identify emerging issues and learning outcomes. This step represents the core of the learning cycle and as such it is important that reflection meetings are held as often as possible, typically every three to six months.

Participants: key decision makers and representatives from stakeholder groups including the local community.

Further Learning Cycles

Not all steps of the LLab process need to be repeated in future cycles. As decision makers and the community become engaged in further cycles of learning, the benefits of the Learning Lab will grow and multiply. This will steadily enlarge the circle of influence of those engaged in this participatory decision-making process to the point where learning becomes institutionalized in the course of the project.

As new stakeholders could join at different stages of the Learning Lab, it may be necessary to repeat the Systems Thinking workshop to build necessary skills and a common language for the participants.

Siem Reap Community Workshop — Identifying Issues

The first workshop of the Siem Reap LLab was conducted in Siem Reap in May 2009. The purpose of this "community" workshop was to identify key issues that the Ministry was grappling with in relation to sustainable tourism. Over 65 participants from the Ministry of Tourism and various relevant departments and organizations in Cambodia attended the workshop. Other senior participants included the Governor of Siem Reap, the

Secretary of State of Tourism, and two senior UNESCO officials. The Minister himself presided over the workshop with facilitation provided by the UQ researchers. The participants were organized into eight groups with six to eight delegates in each group. The workshop process followed these steps:

1. Individual reflection and writing on Post-it notes
2. Affinity groupings of Post-it notes
3. Summary labels for affinity groups
4. Behavior over time charts for key variables
5. Synthesis and debrief

Community Workshop Questions
Two questions were posed to the participants during the full-day workshop.

Q1: What are the barriers/challenges for sustainable tourism for Cambodia?
The delegates responded to this question individually using the silent brainstorming process with sticky notes. This was followed by sharing of issues by each group and open discussion and exchange amongst the participants. This process generated 40 issues which, after combining and removing the duplicates, were reduced to 25 distinct issues as shown in Table 3.

Table 3.   Barriers/challenges for sustainable tourism for Cambodia.

1. Lack of rules and regulations (3 times — mentioned by 3 groups)
2. Lack of law enforcement (3 times)
3. Lack of developed infrastructure (3 times)
4. Lack of coordination (3 times)
5. Lack of capacity building (3 times)
6. Low level of education (2 times)
7. Poverty (2 times)
8. Safety and security (2 times)
9. Sanitation (2 times)
10. Lack of public awareness (2 times)
11. Lack of tourism facilities (2 times)

(Continued)

Table 3. (*Continued*)

12.	Pollution (2 times)
13.	Corruption
14.	Cultural impact (bad influence of tourism)
15.	Lack of understanding of tourism development
16.	Waste management
17.	Quality services
18.	Lack of integrated planning
19.	Lack of local community participation and benefit sharing
20.	Lack of sustainable indicators
21.	Lack of master plan and policies
22.	Economic crisis
23.	Lack of environmental protection
24.	Social and political issues
25.	Lack of urban planning and implementation

It is apparent that the above challenges are not independent or isolated. To demonstrate the complexity and interconnections of these barriers, an initial Causal Loop Diagram (CLD) was constructed and is shown in Appendix 1.

The second workshop question was formulated as:

Q2: What are the drivers/factors that affect sustainable tourism for Cambodia?

A process similar to the one used for Question 1 was followed by the participants, to respond to the second question. This resulted in 29 net factors as shown in Table 4.

Table 4. Drivers/factors affecting sustainable tourism for Cambodia.

1. Infrastructure development (4 times)
2. Increase public awareness (3 times)
3. Political stability (3 times)
4. Government policies (3 times)

(*Continued*)

Table 4. *(Continued)*

5. Set up and implement policies and master plan (2 times)

6. Protection of the environment and sanitation (2 times)

7. Sharing experience and information in seminars and workshops

8. Conservation of natural resources and promotion of local culture

9. Honesty and reasonable prices

10. Sharing tourism income for all

11. International relationships

12. Service quality

13. Encouragement to use local products

14. Equal share of tourism benefits among stakeholders

15. CPP products (conservation, protection, preservation)

16. New products and destinations

17. Increase waste management

18. Security and safety

19. Eco tourism

20. Responsibility of institutions

21. Education (at all levels)

22. Building capacity

23. Broadcast and educate people about eco and sustainable tourism

24. Preserve and develop sustainable tourism with all stakeholders

25. Motivations from government for foreign investors

26. Conservation and development

27. Management

28. Funding

29. Clear understanding of the main barriers

Systems Thinking Training — Building Skills and Capacity

Following the community workshop in Siem Reap, a delegation of 14 managers and staff from the Ministry of Tourism were sent to the University of Queensland in Brisbane for a month-long course of intensive training during October and November 2009. The core component of the training was learning the Systems Thinking concepts and model building skills for group decision making. During this training, using the expert knowledge of the participants, a formal CLD was constructed that embraced the multi-faceted nature of sustainable tourism in the context of Cambodia, as shown in Figure 39.

As can be seen, the CLD model integrates a complex web of relationships connecting social, economic, governance/political, and environmental domains. Four reinforcing vicious cycles (R1 to R4) and one balancing loop (B) are identified in the model (to avoid clutter, link polarities are not shown). In initial discussions, the expert participants unanimously agreed that the potential leverage areas lie in the reinforcing loop R4, showing the insidious links between lack of education, lack of community participation, and poverty. Yet a final decision on the leverage areas was left to the next workshop when a greater cross-section of stakeholders was going to be present.

Systems Workshops — Finding Leverage Areas

The next step of the LLab involved two workshops held in Siem Reap on August 14th and 16th 2010. The first workshop was with high-level managers and officials and the second one was with community representatives and middle-level managers who were to be the implementers of the policies. These workshops were organized under the patronage of the Deputy Prime Minister, President of the National Commission of Cambodia for UNESCO. Once again, the workshops were presided over by the Minister of Tourism in partnership with and the support of the UNESCO office in Cambodia. The workshops were designed and facilitated by the UQ team. The objectives of these workshops were to:

1. Validate the CLD for sustainable tourism that was developed during the training course
2. Understand the interdependencies of the issues and challenges, and the role and responsibility of each stakeholder group
3. Discuss and understand the implications for coordinated strategy
4. Identify key leverage areas for interventions based on the CLD model

The participants

The second workshop was attended by more than 116 people representing seven different ministries (Ministry of Tourism, Ministry of Agriculture, Forestry and Fisheries, Urban and Land Planning, Education, Ministry of

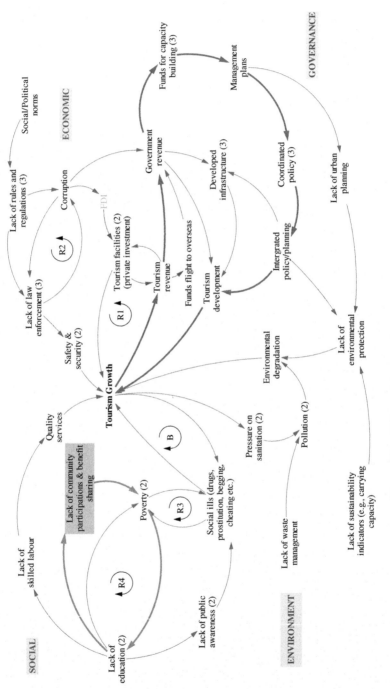

Figure 39. CLD model of sustainable tourism for Cambodia.

Water Resource and Meteorology, etc.), the Tonle Sap Authority, six provinces, community groups, the private sector, and NGOs. As the model integrated social, economic, environmental, and governance dimensions (e.g., integrated planning, law enforcement, political norms) and their interconnections, the research team requested the host Ministry to invite key stakeholders who represented relevant government departments, community groups, NGOs, and provincial governments. This resulted in the large number of delegates.

Such a large group of delegates posed a challenge to the facilitators in running an effective workshop, with discussions being translated into the local languages. This was also a unique opportunity as assembling this number of diverse participants in a single event was rare and precious.

The participants were arranged into 10 groups. The groups represented:

Group 1:	Ministry of Tourism and related institutions
Groups 2, 3, 4, 5, and 7:	Provincial governments
Group 6:	Ministry of Transport
Group 8:	Community representatives from six provinces
Groups 9 and 10:	Private sector

Creating shared understanding

As can be imagined, creating a shared understanding of the issues amongst a group of this size and diversity was a complex task. As discussed earlier, a CLD (systems) model is a powerful and practical visual tool to facilitate this task. For this workshop the CLD model shown in Figure 39 was used as the focal point of discussion within the groups. This model was developed by the research team using barriers and drivers that were identified in the community workshop in May 2009. Additionally, the model had received considerable input and discussion from the Ministry staff who took part in the training course during October and November 2009.

The first part of the workshop was devoted to understanding and verifying of the model by the workshop delegates. This step created a shared understanding of the issues and was completed without significant challenges or resistance to the model. This consensus was reinforced by the facilitators who explained that the model was not intended to be complete

Table 5.   Leverage points/areas for Tonle Sap sustainable tourism.

Leverage areas	Frequency
Poverty alleviation	4
Human resource development	2
Education	1
Service quality	1
Rules and regulations	1
Strategic plan (including eco-friendly solution for the floating village)	1

or perfect, but should provide a big picture of interconnected issues and the areas that different stakeholder groups could influence.

Leverage areas

Having reviewed and discussed the CLD model, the groups discussed the potential leverage areas. A brief introduction to Systems Thinking was used to explain the concept of leverage and the difference between leverage points and quick fixes was emphasized. Surprisingly, despite the cultural and language differences, the participants understood and endorsed the concept of leverage for transformative change.

The list of leverage areas identified by the stakeholders is shown in Table 5. Four of the ten groups recognized **poverty alleviation** as the key leverage area for sustainable tourism. This was followed by human resource development (two groups). Other leverage areas identified were education, service quality, rules and regulations, and the need for a strategic plan (1 group each).

It is important to note that in the first workshop, the participants ranked poverty 7th along with six other barriers. However, in the systems workshop, poverty alleviation was identified as the foremost leverage point for sustainable tourism. The key difference between the two workshops was the use of the CLD model in the second workshop where the participants could see the cause-and-effect links between the barriers and drivers within the entire tourism system (Figure 39). This shift of mental-model is commonly observed in systems thinking workshops where decision makers have the opportunity to view a problem as a system of interconnected elements.

Table 6. Examples of intervention strategies for poverty alleviation in Tonle Sap Region.

Intervention strategy	Actions/Projects/Program	Project team
Provide land	— Provide concession land — Provide land for education	— Government — Local authorities — Relevant ministries (e.g., Education; Land, Urbanization and Construction)
Promote and strengthen the legal system	— Improve law enforcement	— Government — Local authorities
Improve literacy skills	— Literacy training — Skill training in sewing, hairdressing, sculpture, etc.	— Government — Local authorities — Ministry of Education
Build community capacity based on people's needs	— Train the trainers workshops — Exchange programs — Study tours	— Provincial governments — NGOs
Improve standard of living	— Provide loans to the communities to set up small businesses to support the fishing industry	— Local government — Relevant ministries

The participants were then asked to consult within their groups and devise intervention strategies and detailed action plans for implementation. This resulted in ten implementation strategies for the six leverage areas. Five examples of invention strategies for poverty alleviation are shown in Table 6.

Further Steps of the LLab

At the conclusion of the systems workshop (Step 3 of the LLab), the research team passed the management of the LLab to the host institution, the Ministry of Tourism, to conduct the further steps of the LLab (i.e., planning workshops, project selection, implementation, reflection meetings). This handover was anticipated at the outset of the project as by this stage it was expected that the Ministry staff had acquired sufficient knowledge, skills, and experience to manage the process. This capacity building amongst stakeholders was one of the key objectives of the Learning Lab; it enables the empowerment of local stakeholders and allows them to take ownership of and manage future projects.

In general, the management of the LLab could take a variety of forms. For the Siem Reap LLab, a management committee was recommended, comprising representatives from relevant ministries, UNESCO, donor organizations, the private sector, and the local community. The key role of the management committee was to oversee the overall operations of the LLab, namely, to arrange training courses, host reflection meetings, and to monitor and document progress.

Lessons and Conclusions

The first step in any multi-stakeholder situation is to create a shared understanding of the problem amongst the participants. This requires the use of a common language for the diverse participants to be able to communicate effectively and focus on the critical few problems rather than the trivial many. The next crucial step is to create a 'safe' space for open and transparent group conversations without fear of judgement or losing ground. This should facilitate and encourage full and frank participation of all stakeholders.

This case demonstrated the application of Systems Thinking to a complex multi-stakeholder national problem. In the Siem Reap project, Causal Loop Diagrams were used to create a shared understanding of the issues and the identification of core problems. CLDs allowed the participants to view the key drivers and barriers and their interconnections in a single picture. The focus on the cause-effect interconnections facilitated convergence of the views and identification of leverage areas.

As a result, alleviation of poverty emerged as the foremost leverage area, selected as the top priority area by four of the ten stakeholder groups. This caused the authorities to rethink their priorities to a focus on the poor and they even re-labelled the initiative "Pro-poor sustainable tourism". This was a major departure from their original approach to tourism growth as a set of isolated strategies propelled by investments in logistics and infrastructure.

This outcome was consistent with UNESCO's vision for biosphere reserves. According to the Director of Ecological and Earth Sciences at UNESCO:

Each biosphere reserve could be a context-specific experiment in sustainable development at varying scales…. The emphasis, over the next 5–10 years on biosphere reserves as learning laboratories for sustainable development provides interesting opportunities to track such changes in site-specific application of the principle and practices of sustainable development. (p. 118, emphasis added)

Due to the dynamic nature of this approach, knowledge generated from relevant scientific research and monitoring and on-ground experience has an important role to play in informing management actions and policy decisions in response to uncertainty and continuous change…. [Learning Labs could provide] a routine practice for testing the validity of assumptions made with regard to the relationships between conservation and the sustainable use of biodiversity as well as the socio-economic development of communities and people at the local, regional and national levels. (pp. 129–130)

What is envisaged are biosphere laboratories full of on-going experimentation used by national authorities and international policy constituencies… to generate insights and hopefully occasional successes for integrating specific conservation and development agendas (p. 130)[5].

---

[5]Ishwaran, N., Persic, A. and Tri, N.H. (2008) "Concept and practice: the case of UNESCO biosphere reserves", *Int. J. Environment and Sustainable Development*, 7(2), 118–131.

Appendix 1

Initial CLD for Barriers to Sustainable Tourism

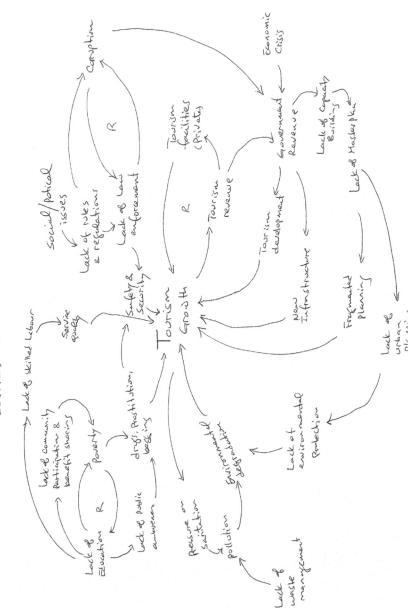

Index

Printed in the United States
By Bookmasters